The Making Of A
Man of God

How David's Process Prepared His Purpose

Author – Eld Joel Latimore Jr.

The Making of a Man of God

How David's Process Prepared His Purpose

Written by Eld Joel Latimore Jr.

© 2025 Eld Joel Latimore Jr.

ISBN (paperback): 979-8-218-86154-4

Latimore Publishing

Scripture quotations are taken from the King James Version (KJV) of the Bible, unless otherwise noted.

Table of Contents

- Dedication

- Author's Note

- Preface

Dedication

To every servant of God who has been anointed in private but tested in public.

To those who fought giants no one saw, and cried tears no one heard.

To the shepherds overlooked by men but chosen by God.

To the worshipers who sang through their sorrow and the warriors who refused to lay down their sword.

To every believer who has been pursued by fear, misunderstood by others, yet preserved by grace— this book is for you.

May the life of David remind you that your cave is not a curse—it is a classroom.

Your tears are not wasted—they are being counted by God.

And your process is not punishment—it is preparation.

Before God placed a crown on David's head, He placed character in his heart.

And He is doing the same for you.

— Eld Joel Latimore Jr.

Author's Note

When I began studying the life of David, I didn't see a perfect man—I saw a process.

A shepherd overlooked, a warrior betrayed, a leader broken, a king forgiven.

What gripped me most was not his anointing but his becoming. The path from pasture to palace was paved with *rejection, isolation, temptation,* and *restoration.* And yet, in each season, God was making a man after His own heart.

This book was written in the same spirit as **The Dream Lives On**—but this time, the focus is not on a dreamer, but on a worshiper.

David's life teaches us that before God gives you a throne, He gives you a test—and before He entrusts you with influence, He walks you through obscurity.

Throughout this journey, you will see how David's Psalms mirror his pain and reveal his progress. The words he penned in *caves, deserts,* and *valleys* are proof that worship is often born in warfare.

Each chapter follows a pattern of *reflection, interpretation*, and *spiritual insight,* blending biblical study with practical application.

My prayer is that this work will read as both a devotion and a sermon, awakening your courage, refining your heart, and reminding you that God never wastes pain.

As you turn these pages, may you feel what David felt—the ache of waiting, the cost of obedience, and the joy of restoration.

And may you know that your own journey, though filled with tests, is not a detour but a divine design.

With love and purpose,

Eld Joel Latimore Jr.

Latimore Publishing

Preface

David's story is the portrait of a man being shaped in the shadows.

Anointed by Samuel in **1 Samuel 16,** David received the oil before he ever received the throne. The crown was delayed not because God had forgotten him, but because God was forming him.

The New Interpreter's Bible Commentary observes that David's narrative displays the irony of grace and discipline—where divine sovereignty works through human weakness to fulfill eternal purpose.

In other words, God was not looking for perfection in David; He was cultivating *submission, trust,* and *humility* through hardship.

Long before David sat on Israel's throne, he learned to bow before God's presence.

Long before he carried the scepter, he carried a sling.

And long before he wore a robe of royalty, he wore the garments of a servant.

Every stage of his life—*the field, the cave, the court*, and *the crown*—revealed another layer of divine preparation.

The pastures trained his hands for worship.

The wilderness trained his heart for war.

The palace tested his integrity.

And the Psalms recorded his transformation.

Psalm 34, written after feigning madness before Abimelech, shows David's resolve to bless the Lord even when humiliated.

Psalm 57, penned in the cave of Adullam, reveals a heart that trusted God while hiding from Saul's spear.

Psalm 51, born from repentance, exposes the broken cry of a king stripped of pride yet restored by mercy.

And **Psalm 142**—*"I cried unto the Lord with my voice"*—echoes from the cave of despair, reminding us that God hears even the whispers of the wounded.

These Psalms remind us that worship is not a sound—it's a surrender.

Faith is not the absence of fear—it's the refusal to stop trusting God in the middle of it.

Like Joseph's journey in **The Dream Lives On,** David's story reminds us that calling comes with conflict, and every promise carries a process. But this time, the focus is deeper—on the interior life of a man whom God shaped from the inside out.

When **The New Interpreter's Bible** describes David's reign, it notes that "the tension between divine promise and human failure becomes the receptacle where covenant faithfulness is revealed."

That's where you and I live—between calling and correction, favor and fire, promise and process.

So, as you read this book, approach it not as a biography, but as a mirror.

Each chapter invites you to see your own journey in David's story—to recognize your caves, your giants, your repentance, and your redemption.

Because the making of a man of God has never been about ease—it's about endurance.

It's not about being flawless; it's about being faithful.

And it's not about reaching the throne; it's about becoming the kind of heart that can carry it.

Before God ever gives you the kingdom, He gives you Himself.

And once you have His presence—you have everything you'll ever need.

— Eld Joel Latimore Jr.

Introduction

Anointed in the Field, Refined in the Fire

Every man and woman called by God will eventually discover this truth: **anointing comes quickly, but becoming takes time.**

When the prophet Samuel poured oil upon the head of young David, it was not a coronation—it was a calling. The oil marked him, but the process would make him.

At that moment, David was still tending sheep, unnoticed by men but already seen by God. His anointing came in obscurity, away from the applause of Israel's army or the prestige of Saul's court. Heaven chose him in a place that smelled like work, wilderness, and worship.

The New Interpreter's Bible Commentary
observes that the narrative of David's anointing
(1 Samuel 16:1–13) reveals God's deliberate
reversal of human expectations. While Jesse
looked at outward stature, God was searching for
inward surrender. The commentary notes that
David's heart—not his height—qualified him for
divine purpose.

*"For the Lord seeth not as man seeth; for man
looketh on the outward appearance, but the Lord
looketh on the heart."* **(1 Samuel 16:7)**

It was in that unseen field that David learned the
rhythms of grace—the patience of waiting, the
courage of obedience, and the discipline of
worship.

The pasture was not his punishment; it was his
preparation.

Hidden Before Honored

Before David faced Goliath, he faced *loneliness.*
Before he conquered kingdoms, *he conquered
fear*. God hid him in the pasture to shape him in
private before displaying him in public.

Every hidden season in David's life was pregnant
with purpose.

The New Interpreter's Bible explains that
God's silence in David's story often signals His
shaping. The absence of visible promotion does
not indicate divine neglect; it reflects heaven's
precision. David's obscurity was God's
classroom—where the lessons of humility,
obedience, and faith were etched into his heart.

While his brothers dismissed him as *"the youngest"* and *"the keeper of the sheep,"* heaven saw a king in training.

The oil of anointing had touched his head, but the call of destiny had yet to be tested in his heart.

Psalm 78:70–72 captures this sacred development: *"He chose David also his servant, and took him from the sheepfolds... to feed Jacob his people, and Israel his inheritance. So he fed them according to the integrity of his heart; and guided them by the skillfulness of his hands."*

Integrity before influence. **Skill** before sovereignty. **Character** before crown.

This is the divine order of preparation.

The Process of Pain and Praise

David's journey from the field to the throne was not a straight path—it wound through *caves, deserts, betrayals,* and *tears.*

He was hunted by Saul, betrayed by friends, disciplined by God, and refined by fire. Yet, in every hardship, David found a way to turn pain into praise.

When he hid in the cave of Adullam, he did not curse his confinement; he composed **Psalm 142:**

"I cried unto the Lord with my voice; with my voice unto the Lord did I make my supplication."

When he fled from Saul into the wilderness of
En-gedi, he penned **Psalm 57:**

*"Be merciful unto me, O God, be merciful unto
me: for my soul trusteth in thee."*

When shame overtook him after sin, he wrote
Psalm 51:

*"Create in me a clean heart, O God; and renew
a right spirit within me."*

And when victory returned to his life, he
declared in **Psalm 18:**

*"It is God that girdeth me with strength, and
maketh my way perfect."*

Each psalm became a record of transformation—
his inner diary of divine dependence.

David's tears watered his testimony. His songs
were not born from triumph but from trial.

In David, we see what **The New Interpreter's
Bible** calls *"the theology of honest worship"*—
faith that is not afraid to lament, to question, or to
cry, yet remains anchored in covenant trust.

The Purpose Behind the Process

Why did God allow so much suffering in the life of a man He had already chosen?

Because calling must be tested before it can be trusted.

David was destined to lead Israel, but before he could guide a nation, he had to be guided by the Spirit. Before he could carry the weight of a crown, he had to bear the weight of rejection.

Every spear that Saul threw, every tear that fell, and every delay David endured was shaping him into a man who could handle both power and purity.

As you read this book, remember: the making of a man or woman of God always involves tension.

- The anointing attracts warfare

.

- The promise invites process.

- And favor always draws fire.

Yet, like David, those who learn to trust God in the cave will one day see His glory in the kingdom.

A Word to the Reader

This is not just a book about David's history—**it is a mirror of your destiny.**

Each chapter will draw from **1** and **2 Samuel, the Psalms**, and **modern commentary** to show how God still develops His servants through *hardship, humility,* and *holiness.*

You will see how divine preparation often hides behind human pain, and how every test— whether in the pasture or the palace—is designed to make you more like Christ.

So, as you read, take your time. Let every lesson sink deep.

Pause between paragraphs. Pray through the Psalms.

Because this is not merely a study—it's a journey.

And on this journey, you will discover that the same God who shaped David through danger and delay is still shaping men and women today—through *process, pain,* and *praise*—until we too become hearts after His own.

Chapter 1 – Anointed but Not Yet Appointed

"And the Lord said unto Samuel, How long wilt thou mourn for Saul, seeing I have rejected him from reigning over Israel? Fill thine horn with oil, and go, I will send thee to Jesse the Bethlehemite: for I have provided me a king among his sons."

— 1 Samuel 16:1

Samuel sat grieving over what was lost. Saul, the man once chosen by God, had disobeyed and fallen from grace. The kingdom looked stable on the outside, but heaven had already declared it empty. Then the word of the Lord came: *"How long will you mourn? Fill your horn with oil and go."*

Those words carried divine urgency—the kind that reminds us that God's purpose keeps moving even when we feel stuck in pain. When one chapter closes, God is already preparing the next.

A Nation Without Reverence

Saul was a man of his generation—raised during the waning days of the Judges, when *"every man did what was right in his own eyes."* Reverence for the Lord had grown *cold,* and *obedience* had become optional. Samuel, the last of the Judges, stood as a lonely voice of holiness in a nation that had forgotten its covenant.

The New Interpreter's Bible Commentary
explains that Saul's rule reflected the disorder of
his age—a leadership built on *image* rather than
intimacy, *command* rather than communion. He
was skilled in strategy but shallow in spirit,
chosen by a people who wanted control more
than consecration.

God needed a different kind of king, one whose
heart had been trained in *the fear of the Lord*. So,
while Saul wore armor, David carried a *harp*.
While Saul sought power, David sought
presence. And in a Bethlehem pasture, a
shepherd's reverence was preparing to replace a
ruler's rebellion.

The Forgotten Command – Torah Reflection

Before Israel ever had a king, the Lord gave clear instructions through Moses:

"And it shall be, when he sitteth upon the throne of his kingdom, that he shall write him a copy of this law in a book out of that which is before the priests the Levites: And it shall be with him, and he shall read therein all the days of his life: that he may learn to fear the Lord his God, to keep all the words of this law and these statutes, to do them."

— Deuteronomy 17:18–19

This command was not ceremonial—it was **spiritual formation.** Every king was to keep a copy of the Law close to his heart so that his reign would remain in reverent submission to God's Word.

But Saul disregarded this completely. He feared the people more than he feared the Lord **(1 Samuel 15:24).** He offered sacrifices unlawfully **(1 Samuel 13:9–12).** He spared what God told him to destroy **(1 Samuel 15:9).** In each act, Saul honored his own logic over God's Law.

According to the covenant, **the king was to rule under Torah, not above it.** Saul's downfall, therefore, wasn't just a matter of bad leadership—it was rebellion against divine order.

David, however, lived in contrast. Though flawed, he cherished the Word. He *hid* it in his heart, *sang* it in his psalms, and *sought* to restore its honor among the people.

"The law of the Lord is perfect, converting the soul… More to be desired are they than gold, yea, than much fine gold." **(Psalm 19:7, 10)**

In David, the command of Deuteronomy was reborn. The boy in the pasture would become a king who loved God's Word, not merely God's position.

Hidden Before Honored

In Bethlehem, in a home that no one thought significant, the prophet found the next king—not among the strong or the tall, but among the humble and unseen. Jesse had sons who looked the part: *Eliab, Abinadab, Shammah*—men of *stature, skill,* and *soldier's build.* But the Lord whispered, *"Look not on his countenance, for I have refused him… for the Lord looks on the heart."*

This first stage teaches us that God's choosing is not based on polish but on purity.

The Lord bypassed seven sons to find one shepherd.

It reminds us that divine calling begins in hidden places where only obedience can be seen.

And somewhere outside, tending sheep, was a young man who didn't even make the guest list.

The New Interpreter's Bible Commentary notes that this moment marked a turning point in Israel's understanding of leadership—from the charisma of Saul to the character of David. God was no longer looking for someone to perform; He was looking for someone to worship.

David was not chosen because he was impressive, but because he was *available.* He wasn't the firstborn, the strongest, or the most experienced—but he was *teachable.* The oil flowed not on the tallest in the house, but on the one who knew how to bow.

And when Samuel anointed him, Scripture says:

"The Spirit of the Lord came upon David from that day forward." **(1 Samuel 16:13)**

Then, surprisingly, David went back to the field.

The anointing came, but the appointment did not.

He had the oil, but not the opportunity.

He had a promise from God—but still had sheep to feed.

The Anointing Stage — Called but Not Crowned

This moment marks **the first stage** of David's development — **the Anointing Stage.**

Before David ever sat upon a throne, he was shaped in secret.

God's anointing always begins in obscurity, not in visibility.

The oil was poured long before the crown was worn.

The Weight of Waiting

That's where many of us live—in that sacred space between what God said and what we see. You've been *called,* but not yet *crowned.* You've been anointed, but not yet appointed.

David's life reminds us that divine delay is not divine denial. The pasture was not punishment; it was process. There, God trained his hands for worship, tuned his ear to hear His voice, and taught his heart to follow.

The pasture is where God builds patience.

It's where He forms character that can carry calling.

It's where He teaches you to shepherd before you rule.

The New Interpreter's Bible notes that David's hidden years shaped the *empathy* and *humility* that would later define his kingship. He learned leadership through loneliness, not limelight.

So, if you find yourself tending *"sheep"*—doing small things with great faith—don't resent it. The same God who called you in private will reveal you in public when the time is right.

Your field is forming your future. Your faithfulness in obscurity will determine your fruitfulness in visibility.

The Breaking of the Outer Man

Before David could lead others, God had to conquer him.

The pasture was not only a classroom — it was a receptacle. There, the outer man was being broken: *the desire to prove himself, the impatience to be seen, the instinct to control his own timing.*

God uses *obscurity* to silence ambition and form surrender. The breaking of the outer man is never meant to destroy; it is meant to release.

As **Watchman Nee** wrote, *"The outward man must be broken before the inward man can serve."*

David's quiet years stripped him of self-dependence. His music came from solitude; his courage was born out of rejection. Before the throne ever fit his shoulders, God was shaping his soul to bear the weight of His glory.

This breaking is painful but necessary — for only the broken can carry the burden of divine power with humility.

Origins of David's Psalms of the Pasture

"The Lord is my shepherd; I shall not want." –
Psalm 23

"Who shall ascend into the hill of the Lord? ...
He that hath clean hands, and a pure heart." –
Psalm 24

Before we hear the beauty of David's worship,
we must remember the barrenness of his
surroundings.

Psalm 23 and **Psalm 24** were not written in royal
comfort; they were conceived in shepherd
solitude.

Psalm 23 – Born in the Fields of Faithfulness

This psalm likely came to life during David's years watching over his father's sheep in the hills outside Bethlehem. There were no crowds, no applause, only stars and sheep — and the steady awareness that God was watching him while no one else did.

When David said, *"The Lord is my shepherd,"* he was not writing theology; he was testifying of daily experience. Every rod, every still water, every dark valley was a memory turned into melody.

It was in that quiet place that David learned dependence — the foundation of all true leadership.

Before he could guide a nation, he had to learn how to follow the unseen Shepherd.

Psalm 24 – Written After Worship

Psalm 24 likely emerged later, perhaps after the Ark of the Covenant was brought back to Jerusalem **(2 Samuel 6).** It celebrates the holiness of God's presence and the purity required to approach it: *"He that hath clean hands, and a pure heart."*

If **Psalm 23** was birthed in solitude, **Psalm 24** was born in sanctuary. One reveals personal devotion; the other public reverence.

Together they form a beautiful symmetry:

- **Psalm 23** shows God's nearness in obscurity.

- **Psalm 24** reveals God's holiness in visibility.

The first was sung to sheep; the second before the sanctuary.

Both show that the breaking of the outer man begins in the field but continues in the temple — until all self-reliance bows to the fear of the Lord.

Stage Insight

The anointing does not crown a man; it begins to crush him.

From this moment forward, David would live between promise and process.

God had chosen him, but the journey to kingship would now expose every flaw and forge every virtue.

Psalmic Reflection – The Heart Before the Crown

"The Lord is my shepherd; I shall not want." – **Psalm 23:1**

"Who shall ascend into the hill of the Lord? ... He that hath clean hands, and a pure heart." – **Psalm 24:3–4**

Before David ever ruled over others, he learned to be ruled by God. **Psalm 23** reflects the peace of the pasture—contentment in God's presence even before promotion. **Psalm 24** reveals the purity required for leadership—clean hands and a heart untainted by ambition.

David wrote these not as a king, but as a servant. He teaches us that worship in obscurity is what prepares you for responsibility. The oil may come in a moment, but the heart must be molded over time.

As **The New Interpreter's Bible** observes, David's psalms transformed private pain into public theology. They prove that the making of a man of God begins long before the throne—it begins in secret places where only God sees.

Wisdom Keys

- God anoints in private before He appoints in public.

- Hidden seasons are holy seasons—embrace them.

- The pasture is where the heart learns humility.

- Every delay is divine development.

- You can be chosen and still waiting—and that's okay.

Reflective Questions:

1. In what ways have I been tempted to honor people's opinions above God's commands, as Saul did?

2. How faithfully do I keep God's Word before me—*reading, meditating,* and *applying* it daily as **Deuteronomy 17:18–19** commands?

3. What *"pasture season"* am I currently in, and what might God be training me to do through it?

4. Am I cultivating a heart that delights in obedience, or one that seeks validation from others?

5. How can I demonstrate reverence for God's Word even in seasons where I feel unseen or uncelebrated?

Reflection Summary:

David's story begins not with power, but with preparation.

He was chosen while still surrounded by sheep.

He was marked by oil before he was recognized by men.

Saul's disobedience teaches us that ignoring the Word leads to instability.

David's reverence teaches us that honoring the Word leads to elevation.

The difference between the two men was **the fear of the Lord**—one lacked it, the other lived by it.

God's pattern has not changed. He still calls us in *secret, tests us in silence,* and *promotes us in His own time.* The pasture teaches dependence; the palace will test it.

If you are in a hidden place, rejoice—it means the Potter still has His hands on you.

David's **first stage — the Anointing Stage —** reminds us that destiny begins with God's choosing, not our earning.

The oil marked him for greatness, but it also marked the beginning of testing.

Every believer anointed for purpose must first learn to walk faithfully in hidden places before they can stand publicly in authority.

But the boy who had been anointed in secret would soon be tested in service.

The field had prepared his hands, but the palace would now test his heart.

Prayer:

Lord,

Thank You for seeing me when others overlook me.

When I grow weary of waiting, remind me that You are still working.

Teach me to be faithful in the field, worshipful in the wilderness, and patient in the process.

Let my heart remain pure, my hands remain clean, and my spirit remain teachable.

Help me love Your Law as David did, and let my reverence for You guide every decision I make.

Prepare me in the pasture for what You've promised in the palace.

In Jesus' name, Amen.

Chapter 2 – The Giant and the Gaze

"Then said David to the Philistine, Thou comest to me with a sword, and with a spear, and with a shield: but I come to thee in the name of the Lord of hosts, the God of the armies of Israel, whom thou hast defied."

— 1 Samuel 17:45

The Apprenticeship Stage — Serving Another Man's Vision

This marked **the second stage** of David's development — **the Apprenticeship Stage.**

The boy who had been anointed in secret was now being observed in service.

God often develops His chosen servants by placing them under imperfect authority.

Before David could lead a nation, he had to learn to serve a king.

Before David ever stood before Goliath, he had already stood before a king. After the anointing, he returned to the pasture until Saul's servants sought a man "cunning in playing."

When David entered the royal court, harp in hand, his music became ministry—soothing Saul's tormented spirit and foreshadowing the worship that would later shake kingdoms.

He learned palace protocol, observed leadership's weaknesses, and gained firsthand experience in the dynamics of authority.

This season prepared him quietly for the public confrontation to come.

By the time the trumpet of war sounded in the Valley of Elah, David's heart had already been trained in both solitude and service.

The battlefield was simply the next classroom in God's school of preparation.

A King's Fear and a Boy's Faith

The Valley of Elah lay between two ridges—
Israel on one side, the Philistines on the other.

For forty days Goliath thundered defiance against
God's people.

But the greater tragedy was not the giant's size—
it was Saul's silence.

The king who once prophesied among prophets
now trembled among soldiers.

This was not a military crisis but a spiritual one. Saul's earlier disobedience had cut off his communion with God, and when fellowship with God breaks, confidence collapses.

As **the New Interpreter's Bible** notes, "Fear replaced faith the moment Saul ceased to seek God's voice. His kingship became a mirror of the nation's unbelief."

When the fear of the Lord departs, the fear of man takes its place.

A guilty conscience cannot stand before a giant. But faith, even in a boy, can move mountains.

The Covenant Perspective

Into this fearful silence stepped a shepherd boy carrying *bread, obedience, revelation,* and *anointing.*

When David heard Goliath's challenge, his heart ignited with holy indignation:

"Who is this uncircumcised Philistine, that he should defy the armies of the living God?"

He wasn't insulting the man—he was exposing his lack of covenant.

David remembered what everyone else had forgotten: no one can defy the people of a covenant-keeping God and win.

Covenant consciousness always conquers fear consciousness.

Faith Founded on the Word

David's courage wasn't spontaneous; it was Scripture remembered.

"For the Lord your God is He that goeth with you, to fight for you against your enemies."

(Deuteronomy 20:4)

He treated that promise as if it had been spoken that morning.

Faith isn't born from emotion but from revelation.

While Saul trusted what he could see—*armor, rank, appearance*—David trusted what he had heard – the Word of God.

Faith fixes its gaze on God, not giants.

Rejecting Saul's Armor

When David volunteered to fight, Saul tried to clothe him with royal armor—an outward solution for an inward problem.

David politely tested it, then shook his head.

"I cannot go with these; for I have not proved them."

The same bronze that covered Goliath now covered Saul. Both trusted in metal; only David trusted in God.

Saul's gesture was more than kindness; it was projection. He was asking David to trust what he himself no longer trusted.

When a man loses intimacy with God, he leans on methods instead of miracles.

David discerned that Saul's armor symbolized misplaced confidence.

He would rather face a giant with God than wear a king's armor without Him.

As **Watchman Nee** wrote, "God cannot use what has not been broken. He breaks the outward man so that the Spirit within may flow freely."

Rejecting the armor was David's first act of spiritual warfare—it was the refusal to copy another man's strength.

Running Toward the Battle

With a sling and five smooth stones, David ran toward Goliath while others hid.

To men it looked reckless; to heaven, righteous.

Invoking the Lord's name, he announced whose authority he stood under. This wasn't a contest of weapons but of worship.

True authority flows from alignment, not achievement.

When the stone struck Goliath's forehead, two things fell—**Goliath's body** and **Saul's illusion of strength.**

The Aftermath – Praise and Peril

The people erupted in praise.

"Saul hath slain his thousands, and David his ten thousands."

They meant no harm, but comparison poisoned the melody.

Words meant as celebration became provocation.

The wounded heart hears comparison louder than praise.

Saul's insecurity turned a joyful song into a personal threat.

Words carry weight; even innocent speech can open doors to envy and division.

Be careful what you celebrate and how you say it—your words can awaken wars you never intended.

The Turning of the Eye

David's trouble with Saul didn't begin with swords — it began with a stare.

The women's song might have stirred Saul's insecurity, but the poison entered the moment he looked at David differently.

"And Saul eyed David from that day and forward." **(1 Samuel 18:9)**

That look marked the start of a slow spiritual corrosion.

Jealousy often begins in silence — in the glances and comparisons that go unrebuked in the heart.

It's the look that says, *"Why him and not me?"*

Observation:

Before Saul ever threw a spear, he threw a look.

And that look was enough to open his heart to suspicion and torment.

Interpretation:

Pride doesn't always shout; sometimes it studies its rival.

Saul's insecurity turned observation into obsession.

Theological Principle:

Jealousy begins with sight before it becomes sin.

Psychological Insight:

Envy magnifies another's favor while minimizing one's own. It whispers comparison until peace is replaced by resentment.

From that day forward, David could feel Saul's eyes before he ever faced Saul's wrath.

This was the true beginning of his suffering — not in open battle, but in quiet betrayal.

The applause of the crowd became the accusation in the king's mind.

Unrecognized by the King

Before the battle, Saul's servants had already described David as *"a mighty valiant man... and the Lord is with him."*

Yet afterward the king asked, *"Whose son is this youth?"*

This wasn't forgetfulness—it was blindness born of pride.

Sin clouds discernment, and pride makes the heart dismissive.

Saul had benefited from David's music yet failed to honor the anointing that soothed him.

- He was not just spiritually blind—he was condescending and look on David and others in contempt.

- He couldn't see greatness in the ordinary because he had learned to judge by status and appearance.

- He forgot that divine favor often wears humble garments.

Pride blinds us not only to God's presence but to God's vessels. The same arrogance that cost Saul his throne now made him overlook the next king standing before him. Sometimes God hides His next move inside the very people pride refuses to see.

"God resists the proud, but gives grace to the humble." **(James 4:6)**

The Breaking of the Outer Man

In the pasture David was broken through waiting; on the battlefield, through warfare.

Every victory exposes something in us that still needs surrender.

The fall of Goliath wasn't David's validation—it was his **initiation.**

Through danger, jealousy, and misunderstanding, God was forming a king before He seated one.

Power without purity becomes corruption; God used pain as preparation.

Psalmic Interlude – Deliver Me from My Enemies (Psalm 59)

When Saul's jealousy erupted, he sent men to watch David's house to kill him

(1 Samuel 19:11–18).

In that fearful night, David's wife Michal helped him escape through a window — and from that place of danger came **Psalm 59.**

Psalm 59 was written during David's early flight from Saul, when he hid in his house as the king's men watched to kill him.

"Deliver me from mine enemies, O my God: defend me from them that rise up against me. Deliver me from the workers of iniquity, and save me from bloody men." **(Psalm 59:1–2)**

This was not the cry of a coward but of a man learning to let God fight his battles.

David had done no wrong, yet he was hunted like a criminal.

In that tension, worship and warfare met. He didn't draw his sword — he raised his song.

"But I will sing of Thy power; yea, I will sing aloud of Thy mercy in the morning."

(Psalm 59:16)

Even while running, he worshiped.

Even while hiding, he hoped.

His instinct was not retaliation but intercession.

He learned that God's mercy is greater than man's malice.

This Psalm shows David's spiritual transformation:

He was no longer fighting with stones, but with surrender.

The outer man was losing comfort; the inner man was gaining confidence.

The boy who once said *"I come to thee in the name of the Lord"* was now learning to wait on the name of the Lord.

Psalm 59 marks the birth of David's mature faith — a faith that trusts God when nothing else makes sense.

The battlefield tested his courage; betrayal tested his character.

This was the breaking point where the shepherd became a vessel.

Psalmic Reflection – Fearless Faith

"The Lord is my light and my salvation; whom shall I fear?" **(Psalm 27:1)**

"Blessed be the Lord my strength, which teacheth my hands to war." **(Psalm 144:1)**

David's gaze was fixed not on Goliath but on God.

Faith founded on the Word produced confidence that fear could not shake.

Every battle became a classroom, every victory a worship service.

Wisdom Keys

- The fear of man is conquered only by the fear of God.

- Borrowed armor cannot win spiritual wars.

- Words can wound even when meant in joy.

- Pride blinds us to divine vessels.

- True victory is when self bows, not just when giants fall.

- Worship is the believer's greatest weapon.

Reflective Questions

1. When have I faced a "giant" that tested what I truly believe about God's power?

2. Have I ever tried to wear someone else's "armor" instead of trusting what God gave me?

3. How have my words—whether in praise, comparison, or reaction—affected those around me?

4. In what ways has pride or insecurity kept me from recognizing God's hand in others?

5. What song or prayer could I lift, like David in **Psalm 59**, when I feel trapped or betrayed?

Reflection Summary:

The pasture taught obedience; the valley taught dependence.

But the hiding place taught endurance.

Saul's fear exposed his distance from the Word, while David's worship revealed devotion to it.

Faith believes what God has spoken; confidence is that faith made visible.

When faith is rooted in the Word, heaven recognizes you—even when men do not.

Prayer:

Lord,

Teach me to trust You when I am unseen, unheard, or misunderstood.

Deliver me from my enemies, both visible and invisible.

Guard my heart from pride and my tongue from harm.

Let my worship rise from the darkest places,

and may every battle draw me closer to Your presence.

Train my hands to war and my heart to worship.

In Jesus' name, Amen.

Chapter 3 – Spears and Separation: The Beginning of Flight

"And Saul cast the javelin; for he said, I will smite David even to the wall. And David avoided out of his presence twice."

— 1 Samuel 18:11

The Adversity Stage — Spears and Separation

This marked **the third stage** of David's development — **the Adversity Stage.**

After serving faithfully under Saul, David entered the season where favor would be tested by fury.

God often allows adversity not to destroy His servants, but to deepen their dependence on Him.

Every calling must pass through conflict.

The Day the Music Turned Dangerous

For a time, David's harp brought peace to Saul's troubled mind.

His melodies quieted the tormenting spirit that came upon the king. But soon, the same sound that soothed Saul began to stir something darker — *jealousy, insecurity,* and *rage.*

It began with a look.

Saul *"eyed David from that day forward,"* and the seed of envy found soil in his heart.

Jealousy never starts with violence — it starts with vision.

It sees what God is doing in someone else and mistakes it as a threat.

The same eyes that once looked upon David with affection now glared with resentment.

Then one day, while David played softly before the throne, Saul's hand tightened around a javelin.

Without warning, the spear flew across the room — not just toward David, but toward destiny itself.

"And Saul cast the javelin; for he said, I will smite David even to the wall."

This was more than an attack—it was an announcement.

The same palace that once celebrated David's anointing would now challenge it. Adversity always exposes what comfort conceals.

God was no longer teaching David how to serve; He was teaching him how to survive.

The one who had once benefited from David's anointing now tried to destroy it.

Saul wasn't fighting David; he was fighting conviction.

Theological Principle:

Jealousy is the flesh's rebellion against divine election.

Saul's problem wasn't David's success — it was God's sovereignty.

He wanted favor without fellowship, position without presence.

But no one can keep what they received by disobedience.

Twice David escaped the javelin.

Each time, God was teaching him:

"No weapon formed against thee shall prosper."
(Isaiah 54:17)

The anointing that empowers also protects.

The Evil Spirit and the Anointed Servant

After Saul's rejection, Scripture says, *"An evil spirit from the Lord troubled him."*

This was not possession, but permission — God allowing Saul's rebellion to bear fruit.

Disobedience opens doors that no man can close except through repentance.

The one who refused to listen to the Spirit now became a vessel for torment.

The peace David carried irritated Saul's unrest.

The anointed will always agitate the afflicted, because obedience exposes rebellion.

Psychological Insight:

When a person has lost the peace of God, they will resent those who still carry it.

That is why Saul wanted to destroy the very presence that once comforted him.

The Table of Tension

David's loyalty never wavered. He served Saul with integrity even after being attacked.

But Saul's heart grew darker.

The final break came during the new moon feast — the king's table, once a place of fellowship, became a place of suspicion.

David discerned the danger and did not attend.

When Saul noticed, his tone turned sharp and accusatory:

"Wherefore cometh not the son of Jesse to meat, neither yesterday nor today?" **(1 Samuel 20:27)**

Jonathan defended David, but Saul's fury exploded.

"And Saul cast a javelin at him to smite him."

(1 Samuel 20:33)

The same weapon that once sought David now sought his defender.

Envy has no loyalty — it consumes everyone in its path.

Jonathan, heartbroken, went out to the field to warn his friend. Their covenant tears marked one of the most sacred moments in Scripture.

The Covenant Between Brothers

"And Jonathan caused David to swear again, because he loved him: for he loved him as his own soul." **(1 Samuel 20:17)**

Jonathan's friendship was a divine gift — a shield between David and destruction.

When Saul's jealousy burned hot, God sent David a friend to stand in the fire with him.

Jonathan risked his life to protect God's chosen.

Their farewell in the field was not a goodbye —
it was a release.

Every anointed person will face a season where
loyalty is tested, friendships are strained, and
motives are purified.

The Adversity Stage is where God prunes the
heart—cutting away dependency on others so
that our confidence may rest solely in Him.

Jonathan would remain in the palace; David
would step into the wilderness.

Both loved by God, yet walking different roads.

David wept until *"he exceeded."* His tears flowed like rivers, not from weakness, but from understanding — God was separating him for something greater.

The spear had not pierced his body, but it had pierced his comfort.

Every spear that missed him was a message from heaven:

"You're not meant to die here — you're meant to grow here."

Spears and Separation

The spear symbolized more than Saul's rage — it represented divine separation.

God was using hostility to move David from the palace to the place of preparation.

Every divine calling requires separation from human comfort.

Before David could rule over Israel, he had to learn to be ruled by God alone.

Sometimes the very thing that wounds you is the hand that moves you.

Rejection becomes relocation; opposition becomes ordination.

Saul's javelin didn't just miss David — it redirected him.

The palace could no longer contain his purpose.

Psalmic Reflection – Deliver Me from My Enemies (Psalm 59)

That night, Saul sent men to David's house to kill him, but Michal helped him escape through a window.

And from that moment of danger came a song that still strengthens the weary:

Psalm 59 was written during David's early flight from Saul, when he hid in his house as the king's men watched to kill him.

"Deliver me from mine enemies, O my God: defend me from them that rise up against me. Deliver me from the workers of iniquity, and save me from bloody men." **(Psalm 59:1–2)**

This was not the cry of a coward — it was the worship of a man who had learned to let God fight for him.

He did not reach for a weapon; he reached for a psalm. He knew that prayer could pierce farther than spears.

"But I will sing of Thy power; yea, I will sing aloud of Thy mercy in the morning."

(Psalm 59:16)

David's instinct was not retaliation but worship. He understood that the safest place for his enemies was in God's hands, not his own.

Faith is not proven by what you fight, but by what you can let God handle.

Psalmic Reflection – When I Am Afraid (Psalm 56)

Later, when David fled to Gath and found himself among the Philistines, fear gripped him again.

He wrote another song of faith:

"What time I am afraid, I will trust in Thee."

(Psalm 56:3)

David was not pretending to be fearless; he was practicing faith.

Real faith does not deny fear — it declares trust in spite of it.

He chose to worship even while afraid, proving that courage is not the absence of fear but obedience in the midst of it.

The Discipline of Survival

David did not have to fight King Saul — he only had to survive him.

God would take care of His anointed.

The battle was not about who would win; it was about who would wait.

Twice David had the chance to kill Saul — once in the cave at En-gedi **(1 Samuel 24)** and again in the hill of Hachilah **(1 Samuel 26).**

Both times he refused.

"The Lord forbid that I should stretch forth mine hand against the Lord's anointed."

(1 Samuel 26:11)

David understood that the one who crowns must be the one who removes.

To strike Saul would have been to step out of God's timing.

This was not cowardice — it was consecration.

David's restraint proved his readiness for the throne.

He didn't need to defend his calling because he trusted the Caller.

Theological Principle:

God will never crown a man who cannot control himself.

Every javelin Saul threw was another opportunity for David to protect his spirit.

He would rather flee than become bitter, rather sing than seek revenge.

His strength was not in his sword — it was in his self-control.

David's survival was not just about staying alive; it was about staying aligned.

He refused to become what he despised.

In sparing Saul, David kept his heart from contamination.

Spiritual Insight:

To fight Saul would have been to fight God's process.

To wait on God was to win without striving.

That is the discipline of survival — trusting that God defends His own anointed.

David didn't have to defeat Saul; he only had to outlast him.

Every day of restraint was a day of refinement.

When the time came, God would remove Saul Himself, and no man could say David's hands were stained.

Patience was David's greatest weapon.

In the waiting, he became the kind of man who could carry a kingdom.

Wisdom Keys

- Envy begins with a look before it becomes a weapon.

- The anointing attracts attack but guarantees divine defense.

- Every spear that misses is another sign that destiny is still intact.

- True friendship stands between wrath and purpose.

- God sometimes uses rejection to reposition His chosen.

- To fight Saul is to forfeit God's timing; to wait is to win.

The Wilderness Principle – When God Develops You

It is incredible how, when God wants to develop you,

He often allows you to see your enemies for who they truly are.

He doesn't reveal them to make you hate them, but to make you holy.

He doesn't expose them so you can fight them, but so you can flee to Him.

God will pull you away from *comfort, familiarity,* and *applause.*

He will allow peace to be disrupted and safety to be stripped away — not because He is angry, but because He is preparing you.

When God is shaping a vessel, He doesn't leave it in the palace; He sends it into pressure.

It's in survival mode that you learn what sustains you.

You pray more earnestly, you worship more honestly, and you depend on Him more completely.

The same God who anointed David in the field was now developing him in the fire.

David's comfort ended, but his calling was just beginning.

He could no longer rely on Saul's favor, Jonathan's friendship, or Michal's protection — he had to rely on God alone.

And that's where true development happens — when God strips away every prop until all you have left is His presence.

Spiritual Insight:

The wilderness is not punishment; it is preparation.

God hides His chosen not to humiliate them, but to shape them.

Before David could wear a crown, he had to survive the cave.

Before he could shepherd a nation, he had to learn to be shepherded by God.

This was not demotion — it was divine development.

Insight from Watchman Nee – The Breaking of the Outer Man

Watchman Nee once wrote that "God must deal with the outer man before the spirit within can be released."

He taught that every servant of God must pass through seasons of crushing—where the outer life of *pride, fear,* and *self-reliance* is shattered—so that the inner life of the Spirit may flow freely.

This is what the wilderness does.

It is God's classroom for breaking the strong will, exposing hidden motives, and emptying the self of dependence on men.

The palace taught David skill; the wilderness taught him submission.

The spear revealed his enemies; the cave revealed his own heart.

Watchman Nee would say that Saul was not simply David's oppressor—he was David's instrument of discipline.

Through Saul, God broke David's outer man, stripping away everything that could not reign with humility.

Only when the self-life is crushed can the fragrance of the Spirit be released.

"Until the outer man is broken," **Nee** wrote, "the inner man cannot be released.

Our environment, our misunderstandings, our trials—these are the chisels of God, cutting away all that hinders the Spirit's flow."

So, the wilderness was mercy, not misery.

God was preparing a king whose authority would come not from the throne, but from a broken and contrite heart.

David's third stage — *the Adversity Stage* — reveals that hardship is often the hammer of holiness.

Before God could trust David with the crown, He had to test him with conflict.

The spears that were meant to destroy him only drove him closer to God.

Adversity is never wasted when it pushes the servant of God deeper into *prayer, worship*, and *dependency.*

The wilderness now awaited David — not as punishment, but as preparation.

Reflective Questions:

1. How do I respond when I'm attacked or misunderstood while walking in obedience?

2. Have I mistaken God's separation for rejection, when in truth He was preparing me for more?

3. What "spears" has God allowed in my life to push me from comfort into calling?

4. Can I trust God enough to defend me, rather than fighting to defend myself?

5. What areas of my life is God placing in "survival mode" to develop spiritual strength and endurance?

Reflection Summary:

David's journey from Saul's court to the wilderness was not a fall from favor — it was the unfolding of formation.

The spears that sought to destroy him only pushed him toward destiny.

Through jealousy, danger, and divine restraint, David learned that the path to the crown runs through caves, tears, and patience.

He did not need to prove himself to men; he needed to be preserved by God.

And in the silence between the throws of Saul's spears, David discovered that sometimes survival is victory.

The same God who preserved David's life in the palace was now training his heart for the throne.

Prayer:

Lord,

Teach me to wait on Your timing and trust Your defense.

When envy rises against me, help me to respond with grace.

When rejection stings, remind me that You are my refuge.

Let me never fight what You are using to form me.

Keep me humble in victory and faithful in hiding.

And may I learn, like David, that to survive is sometimes to triumph.

In Jesus' name, Amen.

Chapter 4 – In the Caves of Formation

"David therefore departed thence, and escaped to the cave of Adullam…"

— 1 Samuel 22:1

The Wilderness Stage — Formation in Isolation

This marked **the fourth stage** of David's development — **the Wilderness Stage.**

Driven from the palace, hunted by the king he once served, David entered God's classroom of solitude.

In this stage, the noise of men fades so the voice of God can be heard.

The wilderness is not punishment; it is preparation.

Before David could shepherd a nation, he had to learn to be shepherded by God.

David's anointing had once opened palace doors; now it pushed him into caves.

But God had not abandoned him — He was forming him.

The cave would become the crucible where character was refined, the place where brokenness turned into intimacy with God.

The Cave of Adullam – God's Classroom of Character

When David fled from Saul, he found refuge in the cave of Adullam — a dark, lonely place outside Judah's borders.

The cave stripped him of everything that once defined him.

No court musicians, no royal meals, no shouts of *"Saul has slain his thousands, and David his ten thousands."*

Just silence, shadows, and the sound of his own thoughts echoing off the cold stone walls.

Psalm 142 was written while David hid in the cave of Adullam **(1 Samuel 22),** this Psalm captures his raw cry for refuge.

"When my spirit was overwhelmed within me, then Thou knewest my path." **(Psalm 142:3)**

This was the classroom of character. The cave dismantled the illusion of self-sufficiency.

Here David learned that leadership is not built on crowds but on communion.

Every cave season dismantles the ego until all that remains is the soul's dependence on God.

Observation:

Adullam was not the end of David's calling; it was the womb of it.

In isolation, he discovered identity.

Interpretation:

When God removes external support, it's not rejection — it's redirection.

He isolates His chosen not to punish but to prepare.

Theological Principle:

God refines the anointed before He releases the appointed.

Stage Insight

The Wilderness Stage is where the heart is purified through pressure.

God uses isolation to clarify identity.

When every support system collapses, the believer discovers that God alone is enough.

Many desire the oil, but few embrace the obscurity that keeps it pure.

This was not the cave of defeat; it was the cave of development.

Every echo of loneliness became an invitation to prayer.

Every tear became incense before God's throne.

And from that darkness, songs began to rise that would later become Scripture.

Psalmic Reflection – Psalm 142: The Cry from the Cave

"I cried unto the Lord with my voice; With my voice unto the Lord did I make my supplication. I poured out my complaint before Him; I shewed before Him my trouble." **(Psalm 142:1–2)**

Psalm 142 is David's heart on paper.

It wasn't written on a throne but in a cave.

He was exhausted, hunted, and abandoned — yet still speaking to God.

It reminds us that even in confinement, communion is possible.

David could not escape Saul, but he could still reach heaven.

"I looked on my right hand, and beheld, but there was no man that would know me... Refuge failed me; no man cared for my soul." **(Psalm 142:4)**

Spiritual Insight:

God sometimes empties our lives of human comfort so that divine comfort may fill the void.

When no man cared for David's soul, God did.

When every refuge failed, the Lord became his refuge.

The cave became the place where David learned that God's presence is enough.

The Gathering of the Distressed (1 Samuel 22:2)

"And every one that was in distress, and every one that was in debt, and every one that was discontented, gathered themselves unto him; and he became a captain over them."

Soon, others found David.

Broken men — fugitives, outcasts, and wanderers — came to the cave for refuge.

What began as isolation turned into leadership.

David's private pain became public purpose.

Even in hiding, the anointing still attracted those who needed guidance.

Observation:

God doesn't wait for our circumstances to improve before He uses us.

He calls us to lead while we're still bleeding.

Interpretation:

The wilderness qualifies a leader by compassion.

David's suffering made him approachable — a man who could rule with empathy.

Theological Principle:

Those who have been broken by life become the best healers of others.

In that cave, God was shaping not just a king, but a shepherd — one who understood the wounded and welcomed the weary.

Psalmic Reflection – Psalm 34: A Song of Deliverance

Composed after his escape from the Philistine city of Gath, this Psalm shows praise rising from fear.

"I will bless the Lord at all times: His praise shall continually be in my mouth." **(Psalm 34:1)**

Written shortly after David escaped danger among the Philistines, this psalm shows that praise is possible even when surrounded by fear.

The same man who once hid in caves now worshiped in them.

David's circumstances didn't change — his perspective did.

"The Lord is nigh unto them that are of a broken heart; and saveth such as be of a contrite spirit."

(Psalm 34:18)

Spiritual Reflection:

Praise in the wilderness is proof of maturity.

When the heart chooses gratitude in isolation, the spirit graduates into deeper faith.

Psalmic Reflection – Psalm 57: Confidence in the Shadows

Penned while hiding in a cave from Saul, this Psalm reveals David's confidence beneath God's wings.

"Be merciful unto me, O God, be merciful unto me: for my soul trusteth in Thee: yea, in the shadow of Thy wings will I make my refuge, until these calamities be overpast." **(Psalm 57:1)**

In the cave, David learned that shadows can also be sacred. The same darkness that once frightened him became a covering for his calling.

The enemy sought him, but God shielded him in obscurity.

Interpretation:

Some seasons are meant to hide you, not harm you.

The cave was not a prison; it was a pause ordained by Providence.

Watchman Nee Insight – The Breaking of the Outer Man

Watchman Nee wrote,

"God must deal with the outer man before the spirit within can be released."

This was David's breaking.

The cave shattered the self-reliance that once rested in skill and strategy.

It broke ambition so that anointing could flow freely.

In isolation, the outer man was broken so the inner man could be strengthened.

Nee's words echo through David's life:

"Until the outer man is broken, the inner man cannot be released."

The cave was not cruelty — it was construction.

Every stone pressed against his soul shaped him into a vessel fit for God's use.

Wisdom Keys

- The wilderness is not the absence of God's favor but the evidence of it.

- Isolation reveals identity; silence teaches surrender.

- Every cave season is preparation for public purpose.

- God hides His greatest treasures before He reveals them.

- The same God who anoints in the field develops in the fire.

Reflective Questions:

1. How do I respond when God moves me from visibility to obscurity?

2. What lessons has isolation taught me about dependence on God?

3. Have I allowed my cave seasons to become classrooms for growth?

4. Who has God sent to me in my own cave — and how am I leading them?

5. Can I still praise God even when I don't see progress?

Reflection Summary:

David's time in the cave was not a retreat — it was a rebirth.

The same God who removed him from Saul's palace was rebuilding him in secret.

In Adullam, God transformed an outlaw into a leader, a soldier into a shepherd, and a fugitive into a father of faith.

Every dark place became a birthplace for divine purpose.

Before David could hold the crown, he had to hold on to God in the cave.

Prayer:

Lord,

Teach me to see Your hand in hidden places.

When I am isolated, help me recognize that I am not abandoned.

Let my cave become a sanctuary of worship and growth.

Break my pride, strengthen my faith, and mold me into a vessel You can use.

May I, like David, emerge from every trial refined, restored, and ready to reign.

In Jesus' name, Amen.

Chapter 5 – Tested in Opportunity

"The Lord forbid that I should do this thing unto my master, the Lord's anointed, to stretch forth mine hand against him, seeing he is the anointed of the Lord."

— 1 Samuel 24:6

The Covenant Stage — Restrained by Reverence

This marked **the fifth stage** of David's development — **the Covenant Stage.**

Having survived the wilderness, David now faced a different kind of battle: the test of restraint.

Many are shaped in suffering, but few are proven in power.

This was not a trial of survival — it was a test of *self-control.*

God had already promised the throne, but David understood that divine promises must never be fulfilled by human impatience.

The same hand that could have struck Saul had to learn the discipline of withholding.

He would not touch what God had anointed, even when that anointing had turned against him.

The Cave of En-Gedi – When Power Meets Principle

David found himself once again in a cave — this time in En-Gedi, surrounded by 600 men who whispered,

"Behold the day of which the Lord said unto thee, Behold, I will deliver thine enemy into thine hand." **(1 Samuel 24:4)**

In the darkness of that cave, Saul entered unaware, and David crept silently behind him.

The moment was ripe for revenge — the one who had hunted him was now helpless before him.

But instead of cutting Saul's life short, David only cut a piece of his robe.

As soon as he did, his heart smote him. Conviction rose like fire within his chest.

He knew what his men did not: that opportunity is not always authorization.

"The Lord forbid that I should stretch forth mine hand against the Lord's anointed."

(1 Samuel 24:6)

Observation:

This was the test of restraint — the measure of maturity.

David's greatness was not revealed by what he conquered, but by what he controlled.

Interpretation:

The true proof of anointing is not how we handle our enemies' attacks, but how we handle our opportunities for revenge.

Theological Principle:

God tests the integrity of His servants not only through adversity, but through advantage.

Stage Insight

This is the stage where covenant replaces convenience.

David's loyalty to God's order was stronger than his desire for vindication.

Even when leadership was unjust, David honored the office because he honored the One who appointed it.

Spiritual Insight:

Reverence is the language of those who walk closely with God.

Those who truly fear Him cannot use the sword of flesh to fulfill the promise of the Spirit.

Every covenant man or woman must learn this discipline — to wait until God's timing aligns with God's purpose.

Psalmic Reflection – Psalm 57: Trust in God's Timing

"Be thou exalted, O God, above the heavens; let thy glory be above all the earth." **(Psalm 57:5)**

Psalm 57, written in this same cave period, reflects David's posture of trust.

He refused to exalt himself — he exalted God instead.

Where others would have shouted, *"Look what I've done,"* David sang, *"Be Thou exalted."*

This psalm reveals that divine restraint produces deeper worship.

When we refuse to act outside of God's will, heaven releases greater peace within our soul.

The Second Opportunity – 1 Samuel 26

Sometime later, David was again presented with the same temptation.

Saul lay sleeping in the camp, and Abishai whispered,

"God hath delivered thine enemy into thine hand this day." **(1 Samuel 26:8)**

Abishai was ready to strike, but David stopped him.

"Destroy him not: for who can stretch forth his hand against the Lord's anointed, and be guiltless?" **(v. 9)**

He refused again, proving that maturity is not a moment but a mindset.

David was not driven by opportunity — he was governed by obedience.

Psychological & Spiritual Insight

The Covenant Stage reveals what we believe about God's *sovereignty*.

When David restrained his hand, he declared by his actions: *"If God put Saul on the throne, then only God can take him down."*

That conviction silenced every carnal argument.

His restraint became worship in motion — an offering of trust laid before the Lord.

Watchman Nee once said:

"If we act on impulse, we violate the principle of resurrection life."

David lived that principle.

He refused to act out of impulse and chose to die to self so that God's promise could rise in His own time.

Psalmic Reflection – Psalm 37: Wait on the Lord

"Fret not thyself because of evildoers, neither be thou envious against the workers of iniquity."

(Psalm 37:1)

"Rest in the Lord, and wait patiently for Him: fret not thyself because of him who prospereth in his way." **(v. 7)**

This psalm, likely written later in reflection, captures the theology of restraint.

Waiting on the Lord is not weakness; it is worship.

David learned that vengeance is the Lord's —
and peace belongs to those who trust His process.

The Covenant Lesson

To live by covenant means to let God defend
your reputation.

It is to surrender the right to retaliate and trust
that God's justice is better than man's revenge.

David's decision not to harm Saul preserved the
purity of his anointing.

By refusing to dishonor Saul, he proved he was
ready to inherit Saul's seat.

Theological Principle:

When you honor what God once anointed, you qualify to receive what He is about to anoint.

Wisdom Keys

- Opportunity is not always authorization.

- Maturity is measured by restraint, not reaction.

- God's promises never need our manipulation.

- Those who fear God can wait for His timing without anxiety.

- Honor is the currency of the kingdom — and those who spend it wisely are never empty-handed.

Saul's Final Breach and the End of Disobedience

While David was proving faithful in restraint, Saul was sealing his fate in rebellion.

Unable to hear from God through prophets, priests, or dreams, Saul turned to the forbidden — he sought counsel from a medium at Endor **(1 Samuel 28).**

In that single act, he broke another of God's laws:

"Regard not them that have familiar spirits… I am the Lord your God." **(Leviticus 19:31)**

This act of desperation revealed a heart completely severed from submission.

The same man who once stood tall among the tribes now bowed before a witch for guidance.

The Spirit that once empowered him had long departed, and now fear became his master.

Observation:

Saul's fall was not sudden — it was progressive disobedience that grew from pride, impatience, and the absence of repentance.

When obedience becomes optional, destruction becomes inevitable.

Interpretation:

God had removed His favor not out of cruelty but out of covenantal justice.

Where Saul disobeyed, David obeyed.

Where Saul grasped for power, David waited in humility.

The contrast between these two men is the contrast between self-will and surrender.

Spiritual Insight:

Rebellion always begins as self-reliance.

It disguises itself as strength but ends in separation.

Those who seek answers outside of God's presence eventually find themselves outside of His protection.

Theological Principle:

God removes those who refuse correction, but preserves those who choose submission.

The Battle of Gilboa – The Consequence of Unrepentance

When the Philistines attacked on Mount Gilboa, Saul's army fell swiftly.

His sons were slain, his armor-bearer died, and the king who once stood head and shoulders above Israel now fell upon his own sword.

The tragedy of Saul's end was not in his death, but in his distance from God.

His crown was lost not to the enemy's strength, but to his own stubbornness.

He died the way he lived — fighting battles that obedience could have prevented.

Spiritual Reflection:

There is a warning here for every leader, every believer, and every man of God:

Anointing is not immunity.

No matter how high God lifts us, we must remain low before Him.

David's life rose because he humbled himself; Saul's life fell because he exalted himself.

Contrast in Covenant

At the same time Saul was falling by the sword, David was rising in favor.

The man who refused to take Saul's life would now inherit Saul's throne.

God's justice and mercy intersected on that battlefield — the proud were brought low, and the humble were exalted.

Theological Principle:

The kingdom of God always passes from the disobedient to the obedient.

Reflective Questions:

1. When God gives me the opportunity to *"fix"* a situation in my own strength, do I wait for His timing—or act out of emotion or pride?

2. Do I honor God's order and authority even when leadership fails, disappoints, or mistreats me?

3. In moments of power or advantage, do I seek my own vindication—or God's glorification?

4. What signs in my life show I am responding like David, and what signs warn me I may be drifting into Saul's mindset of self-reliance and spiritual stubbornness?

5. When God seems silent, do I seek Him more fervently—or am I tempted to turn to "other sources" (my own ideas, flesh, worldly counsel, retaliation, manipulation) instead of waiting on Him?

Reflection Summary:

David's test in the cave of En-Gedi revealed more than character — it revealed covenant.

He was no longer reacting to Saul; he was responding to God.

His anointing was being refined through obedience, not through opportunity.

By sparing Saul, David showed that greatness is not found in power but in principle.

The man who refused to take a throne before its time was now ready to receive it in God's time.

Prayer:

Lord,

Teach me to wait with worship instead of impatience.

When opportunity tempts me to act outside Your will, remind me that obedience is greater than outcome.

Give me the heart of David — one that fears You more than it desires vindication.

Let restraint become my testimony and reverence my reward.

In Jesus' name, Amen.

Chapter 6 – The Crown and the Cost

"And the men of Judah came, and there they anointed David king over the house of Judah."

— 2 Samuel 2:4

The Leadership Stage — The Crown and the Cost

This marked **the sixth stage** of David's development — **the Leadership Stage.**

The shepherd boy had finally become king, but not over all Israel.

God had fulfilled part of the promise, not the whole.

And in that in-between place, David would face another test — *the test of patience, stewardship, and spiritual maturity.*

The anointing that once flowed in Bethlehem now rested upon a throne in Hebron.

But though the oil had dried upon his head, the process was still unfolding.

It is one thing to wait for the promise; it is another to govern faithfully while it's only half-fulfilled.

The Amalekite's Lie — A Test of Reverence

When news of Saul's death reached Ziklag, a young Amalekite arrived carrying the fallen king's crown and bracelet.

He claimed that he had ended Saul's suffering on Mount Gilboa and expected David's gratitude — perhaps even reward for finishing off his enemy.

But David's heart broke instead of swelling with pride.

"How wast thou not afraid to stretch forth thine hand to destroy the Lord's anointed?"

(2 Samuel 1:14)

Tearing his garments, David and his men wept and fasted for Saul and for Jonathan.

Then he commanded that the Amalekite be struck down.

Perhaps, as the young man fell, David remembered that moment in the cave of En-Gedi — when his own heart smote him for cutting the edge of Saul's robe.

Now he faced someone who had taken Saul's life and felt no conviction.

The difference was not in the act but in the heart: David's conscience trembled; the Amalekite's was seared.

Spiritual Insight:

Reverence for God's order must remain even when His plan seems delayed.

What we fear to touch in reverence, others may destroy in presumption. The fear of the Lord distinguishes the anointed from the ambitious.

Theological Principle:

God measures a man's maturity not by what he touches, but by what touches his heart. This moment revealed that David's fear of the Lord had not weakened with victory — it had deepened.

Before he ever ruled a tribe, he reaffirmed that reverence would rule his life.

From Hebron to Jerusalem — The Call to Unify

David's rise to kingship began not with full sovereignty but with partial authority.

At Hebron, he was crowned king over Judah alone **(2 Samuel 2:4).**

Meanwhile, Saul's son **Ishbosheth,** sustained by the general **Abner,** ruled the northern tribes of Israel.

The nation remained divided — Judah under David, and Israel under Ishbosheth — for more than seven years.

It was a season of partial fulfillment, a prolonged test of patience.

Spiritual Insight:

God sometimes gives us a portion of the promise to test our posture.

He lets us taste promotion without possessing it fully — not to tease us, but to teach us.

If we cannot handle the portion with humility, we are not ready for the whole.

Observation:

David did not fight to seize what God had not yet released.

He ruled Judah faithfully, waiting for God to unite the tribes in His timing.

Interpretation:

This was divine delay, not denial.

God was still aligning hearts, breaking strongholds, and preparing the nation for unity under a man after His own heart.

Theological Principle:

Every partial promise is a test of patience; how you handle the portion determines whether you're ready for the whole.

Only after Ishbosheth's downfall and Abner's death did all Israel come to David, saying,

"We are thy bone and thy flesh... Behold, we are come to make thee king over all Israel."

(2 Samuel 5:1–3)

Then, at last, the divided kingdom became one, and David reigned over the entire nation for thirty-three more years.

The Murder of Ishbosheth — A Test of Integrity

Not long after, two brothers named **Rechab** and **Baanah** entered the house of Ishbosheth, Saul's son, and murdered him in his sleep.

They brought his head to David, saying,

"Behold the head of Ishbosheth… the Lord hath avenged my lord the king this day of Saul and of his seed." **(2 Samuel 4:8)**

But David once again refused to rejoice in bloodshed done in his name.

He replied,

"When one told me, saying, 'Behold, Saul is dead,' thinking to have brought good tidings, I slew him... How much more, when wicked men have slain a righteous person in his own house upon his bed?" **(2 Samuel 4:10–11)**

He ordered their execution and honored Ishbosheth with burial.

Spiritual Insight:

David's rise to power was marked by restraint, not revenge.

He refused to build his kingdom on treachery.

He knew that what begins in manipulation must be maintained by manipulation — but what begins in righteousness will be sustained by God.

Theological Principle:

When God promises a throne, He does not need the help of wicked hands to secure it.

Stage Insight

The Leadership Stage is not the end of development — it's the beginning of stewardship.

The throne reveals what the wilderness refined.

God had shaped David's hands for war, but now He would shape his heart for wisdom.

Power is the final test of purity.

Spiritual Insight:

The higher God lifts you, the more you must bow before Him.

Every crown carries weight, and every promotion demands deeper prayer.

Psalmic Reflection – Psalm 18: Praise for Deliverance

"It is God that girdeth me with strength, and maketh my way perfect. He teacheth my hands to war, so that a bow of steel is broken by mine arms."

— Psalm 18:32–34

Psalm 18 was written when the Lord had delivered David from Saul and his enemies, yet before his reign reached full unity.

Even in partial fulfillment, David worshiped as though the promise were complete.

He understood that praise is not reserved for final victory; it belongs in every phase of progress.

168

Interpretation:

Gratitude in transition is the mark of maturity.

When David sang in Hebron, he wasn't thanking God for the throne alone — he was thanking Him for the process that led there.

Theological Principle:

Those who praise in partial fulfillment position themselves for full inheritance.

The Cost of the Crown

Power carries pressure.

Leadership demands listening.

David's days of hiding were over, but his nights of intercession had just begun.

He now bore the burden of a *divided people, political tension,* and *personal loss.*

Each morning, he rose to the sound of servants, but each evening he knelt before the Sovereign.

Observation:

Leadership reveals the limits of human strength and the necessity of divine guidance.

Interpretation:

God does not call leaders to be perfect; He calls them to be pliable.

Those who stay flexible before the Spirit stay fruitful before men.

Theological Principle:

God gives crowns to servants, not to seekers of status.

Psalmic Reflection – Psalm 101: A Leader's Commitment

"I will behave myself wisely in a perfect way. O when wilt Thou come unto me? I will walk within my house with a perfect heart."

— Psalm 101:2

Psalm 101 is David's royal pledge — a vow to lead with integrity both in public and in private.

He understood that the character of a king shapes the culture of a kingdom.

The throne is holy ground; it must be governed by holiness.

Spiritual Insight:

Public victory means nothing if private virtue is compromised.

David knew that the same God who anointed him expected him to live like he still needed that anointing every day.

Psychological and Spiritual Insight

Leadership exposes what the wilderness prepared.

The applause of men can drown the whisper of God if the heart is not anchored in humility.

David's secret was simple: he never outgrew the posture of a worshiper.

Even when wearing the crown, he remained a man after God's own heart.

Spiritual Principle:

Greatness is sustained only by gratitude.

Wisdom Keys

- The crown does not complete the calling; it enlarges it.

- Partial fulfillment is preparation for full responsibility.

- Every elevation requires deeper consecration.

- God honors leaders who govern with humility and purity.

- The secret to lasting success is remaining small before God even when great before men.

Reflective Questions:

1. How do I respond when God fulfills only part of His promise to me?

2. Do I remain faithful with the portion, or frustrated by what I lack?

3. What spiritual disciplines keep me humble in seasons of success?

4. How do I lead with integrity when influence increases?

5. Can I praise God in transition as passionately as I did in trial?

Reflection Summary:

David's rise to the throne was not instant — it was incremental.

From Judah to all Israel, from partial rule to full reign, every delay was divine design.

He learned that true leadership is not about claiming what's promised, but about caring for what's entrusted.

God measured his faithfulness in the fraction before granting him the fullness.

The crown did not end the process — it revealed its purpose.

God had made not just a king, but a keeper of His presence.

Prayer:

Lord,

When You promote me, preserve me.

Teach me to see partial blessings as full reasons for praise.

Keep my heart pure when power increases, and my eyes fixed on You when influence expands.

Help me to rule my spirit before I rule anything else.

Let every crown remind me of the cost of obedience.

In Jesus' name, Amen.

Chapter 7 – The Heart of Worship: Dancing Before the Ark

"So David and all the house of Israel brought up the ark of the Lord with shouting, and with the sound of the trumpet."

— 2 Samuel 6:15

The Devotion Stage — Presence over Position

This marked **the seventh stage** of David's development—**the Devotion Stage.**

The man who once ruled with courage now had to learn to worship with humility.

God had given him the throne, but David understood that the throne meant nothing without the Presence of the Lord.

Leadership had crowned him; worship would keep him.

Before David could rule successfully from Jerusalem, he needed to center the nation around the Ark—the visible symbol of God's covenant.

It was not military victory that established Israel's strength; it was spiritual order.

Spiritual Insight:

The presence of God is not a decoration in the kingdom—it is the kingdom.

Without His presence, authority becomes empty performance.

A Good Intention Done the Wrong Way

David's first attempt to bring the Ark to Jerusalem was sincere, but misguided.

He placed it on a new cart, drawn by oxen, instead of having the Levites carry it on their shoulders as God's Law commanded

(Numbers 4:15).

When the oxen stumbled and Uzzah reached out to steady the Ark, he was struck dead.

David was grieved and afraid.

"How shall the Ark of the Lord come to me?"

(2 Samuel 6:9)

He left it in the house of **Obed-Edom,** where the blessing of God overflowed for three months.

Observation:

A pure motive cannot excuse a wrong method.

Obedience is the language of love.

Interpretation:

David's enthusiasm was right, but his execution was wrong.

He learned that worship must follow divine instruction, not personal excitement.

Theological Principle:

God's work must always be done God's way.

Spiritual Insight:

When zeal outruns knowledge, even worship can become dangerous.

Returning to the Word

After studying the Law, David realized his error.

He called the priests and Levites to sanctify themselves and carry the Ark properly.

This time, the movement was not just national— it was spiritual.

Every six steps, they stopped and offered sacrifices.

David himself wore a linen ephod—the garment of a servant, not a king.

He laid aside his royal robe because no man is royal before the presence of the Most High.

Observation:

True worship strips away titles and status until only surrender remains.

Interpretation:

David's strength was not in his sword or crown—it was in his surrender.

Theological Principle:

The more God exalts you, the more He expects humility from you.

Dancing Before the Lord

As the procession entered Jerusalem, David could no longer contain his joy.

He danced with all his might before the Lord, leaping, spinning, shouting—unashamed and unrestrained.

The people rejoiced, but not everyone celebrated.

From her window, **Michal,** Saul's daughter, looked down in disdain.

"How glorious was the king of Israel today, who uncovered himself before the handmaids of his servants!" **(2 Samuel 6:20)**

Her words carried contempt.

She saw his worship as undignified.

But David replied,

"It was before the Lord... therefore will I play before the Lord. And I will yet be more vile than thus." **(2 Samuel 6:21–22)**

Spiritual Insight:

When pride refuses to bow, worship looks foolish.

When humility bows low, glory fills the room.

Psychological Insight:

Michal valued reputation; David valued relationship.

Those who live for approval can never enter abandoned worship.

Theological Principle:

God shares His glory with the humble, not the self-conscious.

Psalmic Reflection — Psalm 24: The King of Glory

"Lift up your heads, O ye gates; and be ye lift up, ye everlasting doors; and the King of Glory shall come in." **(Psalm 24:7)**

Many scholars believe **Psalm 24** was written for this very occasion—the Ark entering Jerusalem.

The psalm asks, *"Who shall ascend into the hill of the Lord?"* and answers, *"He that hath clean hands and a pure heart."*

David knew that external worship must flow from internal purity.

Interpretation:

The King of Glory enters only through clean hearts.

Worship opens what pride keeps shut.

Spiritual Principle:

The doors that refuse praise will never host Presence.

Stage Insight

The Devotion Stage teaches that ruling God's people requires remaining ruled by God's Presence.

Every victory must lead back to worship; every success must end in surrender.

David's reign would be remembered not for wealth or armies, but for his songs.

Spiritual Insight:

Worship is not a break from leadership—it is the breath of it.

Wisdom Keys

- The presence of God is more vital than the position of power.

- Zeal without obedience brings danger, not delight.

- Humility is heaven's dress code.

- Worship exposes pride and expands peace.

- Every blessing increases responsibility to honor the Blesser.

Reflective Questions:

1. Do I serve God with enthusiasm but neglect His instructions?

2. How do I respond when correction interrupts my worship?

3. Have I allowed pride to make me too dignified to dance before the Lord?

4. In what ways can I prioritize Presence over performance?

5. What does authentic worship look like for me today?

Reflection Summary:

David learned that leadership without Presence is lifeless.

His crown gained meaning only when laid before the Ark.

Worship realigned his motives, renewed his joy, and re-centered the nation around God.

He discovered that the true strength of Israel was not in armies or walls—but in adoration.

When the King bowed, the kingdom was blessed.

Prayer:

Lord,

Teach me to worship like David—with reverence, joy, and surrender.

Strip away my titles, fears, and pride until only Your presence matters.

Let obedience guide my zeal and humility govern my heart.

May every victory lead me back to Your feet.

You are the King of Glory; enter my life again today.

In Jesus' name, Amen.

Chapter 8 – Blessing and Boundaries: The Covenant with God

"Also the Lord telleth thee that He will make thee an house."

— 2 Samuel 7:11

The Covenant Stage — Promise through Restraint

This marked **the eighth stage** of David's development—**the Covenant Stage.**

The man who once fought for survival and later danced for presence now stood in a new classroom of grace: learning to be blessed while still bound by God's will.

At last, the kingdom was united, the Ark rested in Jerusalem, and peace surrounded him. David's heart overflowed with gratitude and vision. He looked around at his cedar palace and said to the prophet Nathan,

"See now, I dwell in an house of cedar, but the ark of God dwelleth within curtains."

(2 Samuel 7:2)

He longed to build God a permanent dwelling—a place that reflected honor and stability.

But that night, God sent word through Nathan:

"Thou shalt not build Me an house to dwell in… the Lord will make thee an house."

(2 Samuel 7:5 – 11)

When God Says "No" to a Good Thing

David's desire was sincere, but God's denial was sovereign.

The warrior-king would not be the builder-king. His hands had shed too much blood **(1 Chronicles 28:3).** The task would fall to his son, Solomon.

Observation:

Sometimes God denies our dreams not because they are evil, but because they exceed our season.

Interpretation:

David's rejection was not punishment—it was redirection. God was teaching him that favor must live within the framework of obedience.

Spiritual Insight:

The true test of maturity is how we respond when God says "no."

Will we pout—or will we praise?

Theological Principle:

Every divine "No" contains a deeper "Yes" to God's purpose.

God's Covenant — Blessing Beyond Building

Instead of allowing David to build a physical house, God promised to build him a spiritual dynasty.

"I will set up thy seed after thee… and I will establish the throne of his kingdom for ever."

(2 Samuel 7:12 – 13)

This was more than a royal decree—it was the birth of the Davidic Covenant, fulfilled ultimately in **Jesus Christ, the Son of David.**

David had wanted to make a home for God; God promised to make an eternal home through David.

Observation:

God always outgives the giver.

Interpretation:

What David offered was temporary; what God established was eternal.

Theological Principle:

You cannot outbuild the Builder of heaven and earth.

Spiritual Insight:

David learned that obedience produces legacy. The blessing of God is not earned by works but entrusted through worship and submission.

David's Prayer of Humility

When David heard God's promise, he went in and sat before the Lord—astonished, humbled, and undone.

"Who am I, O Lord God, and what is my house, that Thou hast brought me hitherto?"

(2 Samuel 7:18)

He didn't argue; he adored. He didn't negotiate; he knelt.

His response models the proper posture of a blessed heart: awe, not arrogance.

Psychological and Spiritual Insight:

Gratitude resets the soul.

David's humility revealed that true greatness bows even under glory.

Theological Principle:

The covenant was not made with a perfect man but with a worshipping one.

Psalmic Reflection — Psalm 132: A Heart for God's House

"Surely I will not come into the tabernacle of my house, nor go up into my bed; I will not give sleep to mine eyes… until I find out a place for the Lord."

(Psalm 132: 3 – 5)

Psalm 132 captures David's consuming desire to establish a resting place for God. It reflects both his zeal and his surrender—the balance between passion and patience.

Interpretation:

God honors hearts that yearn for His dwelling, even when He redirects their hands.

Spiritual Principle:

God sometimes fulfills your prayer through someone you raise, not something you do.

Mephibosheth — Covenant in Action

The covenant God made with David soon found its reflection in David's treatment of Saul's crippled grandson, **Mephibosheth.**

This encounter, recorded in **2 Samuel 9**, reveals that divine covenant produces human compassion.

Years after David's throne was secure, he asked,

"Is there yet any that is left of the house of Saul, that I may show him kindness for Jonathan's sake?" **(2 Samuel 9: 1)**

The word kindness here is **ḥesed**—the same covenant love God had shown to David.

Mephibosheth, lame in both feet, lived in fear and obscurity in Lo-debar, a barren land whose name means *"no pasture."*

When summoned before the king, he bowed low and said,

"What is thy servant, that thou shouldest look upon such a dead dog as I am?" **(2 Samuel 9: 8)**

But David raised him up. He restored to him all of Saul's land and commanded that he eat continually at the king's table.

Observation:

Mercy is the visible fruit of covenant.

Interpretation:

David did for Mephibosheth what God had done for him—lifted him from obscurity and seated him in favor.

Spiritual Insight:

Those who have received mercy should never withhold it.

When you truly understand covenant, you stop treating grace as optional.

Theological Principle:

Covenant love finds its proof not in words, but in kindness.

David kept covenant with Jonathan's house because he had learned how faithfully God kept covenant with his.

Psychological and Spiritual Reflection:

Mephibosheth represents all of us—broken, undeserving, and carried by grace to a table we didn't earn.

Stage Insight

The Covenant Stage shows that blessings come with boundaries.

Divine favor must remain under divine order.

David discovered that even when he could not do what he desired, he could still become what God required: **a man after His own heart.**

He prepared materials, wrote psalms, trained Levites, and organized worship teams for the temple his son would build.

He could not construct the structure—but he could cultivate the spirit.

And when God's covenant love filled his heart, it overflowed into his actions toward **Mephibosheth**—proof that the heart of a true king is compassion.

Spiritual Insight:

God may not let you finish every dream, but He will let you form the foundation.

Wisdom Keys

- God's "No" is never rejection; it's redirection.

- Legacy matters more than achievement.

- Blessing without boundaries breeds destruction.

- Obedience keeps favor from turning into idolatry.

- True covenant always extends kindness to others.

- Gratitude is the only right response to grace.

Reflective Questions:

1. How do I respond when God delays or denies my good plans?

2. What boundaries has God placed around my blessings?

3. Do I love God's presence enough to serve His plan, even if I'm not the center of it?

4. Who is God calling me to show covenant kindness to?

5. In what ways can I honor God's covenant through daily obedience?

Reflection Summary:

David's deepest development came not through battle but through balance.

He learned that God's favor doesn't always look like permission; sometimes it looks like restraint.

By accepting divine limits, he gained divine legacy.

The man who once cried in caves now worshipped in covenant—and showed mercy to a crippled descendant of his enemy.

His throne became a table of grace, foreshadowing the greater Son of David who would one day invite the lame, the lost, and the lowly to dine eternally in the Father's house.

Prayer:

Lord,

Teach me to cherish Your "No" as much as Your "Yes."

Remind me that every boundary You set protects the blessing You've planned.

Help me serve faithfully in my season and extend mercy as freely as You have given it.

Build in me a heart that lasts longer than anything my hands could make.

In Jesus' name, Amen.

Chapter 9 – Kindness and Kingship: The Fruit of Covenant Grace

"Then the king said, Is there not yet any of the house of Saul, that I may show the kindness of God unto him?"

— 2 Samuel 9:3

The Mercy and the Measure of a King

This marked **the ninth stage** of David's development—**the Kindness Stage.**

After years of war, victory, and covenant, David entered a new test of leadership—not through battlefields, but through moral balance.

He would learn that the same hand that extends mercy must sometimes uphold justice.

Both belong to the heart of God.

True kingship is not proven by power but by principle.

The one who reigns well must learn when to spare life and when to surrender it in obedience to divine righteousness.

Mercy to Mephibosheth — Covenant Remembered

When peace finally filled the land, David's thoughts turned again to covenant.

He remembered his promise to Jonathan and asked,

"Is there yet any that is left of the house of Saul, that I may show him kindness for Jonathan's sake?" **(2 Samuel 9: 1)**

The answer came: *"Behold, there is yet a son of Jonathan, which is lame on his feet."* **(v. 3)**

Mephibosheth, living in the barren place of Lo-debar, was summoned to the king's palace.

Fearfully, he bowed low before David. But instead of vengeance, he found grace.

"Fear not; for I will surely show thee kindness for Jonathan thy father's sake, and will restore thee all the land of Saul thy father; and thou shalt eat bread at my table continually."

(2 Samuel 9:7)

Observation:

Mercy remembers covenant even when the covenant partner cannot.

Interpretation:

David's act mirrored the heart of God, who lifts the fallen and restores the undeserving.

Theological Principle:

Covenant kindness is not based on merit but on memory—God's remembrance of His promise.

Spiritual Insight:

Every time Mephibosheth sat at David's table, his crippled feet were hidden beneath the king's covering.

That table was not just furniture—it was forgiveness made visible.

The Famine and the Gibeonites — Justice Demanded

Years later, another test arose that revealed the other side of David's covenant duty.

A severe famine struck the land for three consecutive years.

When David sought the Lord, the answer was shocking:

"It is for Saul, and for his bloody house, because he slew the Gibeonites." **(2 Samuel 21:1)**

Saul had violated Israel's covenant with the Gibeonites made in the days of Joshua.

Because of that broken oath, the nation bore the weight of divine displeasure.

David called the Gibeonites and asked what would satisfy justice. They said,

"Let seven men of his sons be delivered unto us, and we will hang them up unto the Lord." **(v. 6)**

David consented. Yet in a striking act of mercy, he spared **Mephibosheth**—Jonathan's son—for covenant's sake.

He delivered seven other descendants of Saul into the Gibeonites' hands, and they were executed on the hill before the Lord.

Only then did the famine cease.

Observation:

The same king who had shown kindness now had to enforce covenant justice.

Interpretation:

David's mercy was never weakness, and his justice was never cruelty.

He understood that grace without righteousness becomes corruption, and righteousness without grace becomes cruelty.

Theological Principle:

The fear of the Lord establishes the balance between mercy and justice.

Spiritual Insight:

God's covenant includes kindness, but it also demands holiness.

David could not let compassion override covenant law—because disobedience in mercy is still disobedience.

Mercy and Judgment in Balance

David's decision cost him emotionally.

He had to carry the grief of obedience—the pain of doing right when it feels wrong.

True leaders know that holiness sometimes hurts.

Afterward, David retrieved the bones of Saul and Jonathan, buried them honorably, and brought closure to an old curse.

Only then did the rain return to the land—a symbol that God's favor had been restored.

Psychological and Spiritual Insight:

Sometimes restoration requires reckoning.

Before God sends new rain, He often deals with old wrongs.

Psalmic Reflection — Psalm 85: Mercy and Truth Meet Together

"Mercy and truth are met together; righteousness and peace have kissed each other." **(Psalm 85:10)**

This psalm perfectly summarizes the tension of David's covenant stage.

Mercy and truth are not enemies—they are companions.

Justice without mercy destroys; mercy without justice deceives.

But in the heart of God—and in the mature heart of His servant—they unite.

Theological Principle:

The throne of God is established on righteousness and justice, but it is surrounded by mercy.

Stage Insight

The Covenant Stage was not only about receiving promises but about walking in their weight.

Every covenant has both privilege and price.

David's kindness to **Mephibosheth** showed the sweetness of covenant; his surrender of Saul's grandsons showed its seriousness.

Both acts revealed that David's heart belonged not to emotion, but to obedience.

He ruled not by impulse but by instruction.

This is the balance of a true man of God—soft enough to show compassion, yet strong enough to uphold holiness.

Spiritual Insight:

When God matures a leader, He teaches him to hold mercy in one hand and justice in the other.

Wisdom Keys

- True covenant requires both kindness and accountability.

- Mercy without truth is false grace; truth without mercy is hard law.

- Leadership means grieving obedience, not comfortable compromise.

- Restoration often requires reckoning before renewal.

- God's mercy never cancels His holiness— it completes it.

Reflective Questions:

1. How do I respond when obedience costs me emotionally?

2. Am I willing to balance mercy and justice in my relationships?

3. Do I protect my covenants, even when others break theirs?

4. How can I show grace without compromising God's truth?

5. What unfinished wrongs in my life might God be asking me to make right?

Reflection Summary:

In this stage of David's life, the covenant matured from promise to principle.

He learned that the same God who extends mercy also enforces justice.

By sparing Mephibosheth, David displayed compassion.

By surrendering Saul's guilty descendants, he demonstrated righteousness.

Only when mercy and truth met together did peace return to Israel.

In this, David foreshadowed the greater King to come—**Jesus Christ**—where ultimate mercy and perfect justice would meet forever at the cross.

Prayer:

Lord,

Teach me to walk in covenant balance—merciful in heart, righteous in action.

Help me obey You even when obedience costs me something dear.

Keep me from sentimentality that excuses sin, and from severity that forgets grace.

May Your mercy and truth meet together in me.

In Jesus' name, Amen.

Chapter 10 – The Return to the Wilderness: Absalom's Rebellion and David's Refining

"And David said unto all his servants that were with him at Jerusalem, Arise, and let us flee; for we shall not else escape from Absalom."

— 2 Samuel 15:14

The Refinement Stage — When God Restarts the Process

This marked **the tenth stage** of David's development—**the Refinement Stage.**

Though he was now a seasoned king, David was not finished growing.

The same God who trained him in Saul's wilderness now brought him into another—one birthed not from persecution, but from consequence.

This time, the enemy was not Saul—but his own son, Absalom.

The Seeds of Rebellion

Years earlier, David had sinned with Bathsheba and orchestrated the death of her husband, Uriah. Though God forgave him, the prophet Nathan warned that the sword would not depart from his house **(2 Samuel 12:10).**

Absalom, his third son, had long been bitter over the rape of his sister **Tamar** by their half-brother **Amnon**—and David's failure to act.

When Absalom took vengeance by killing Amnon, David's heart broke, yet he struggled to discipline him. This unresolved tension created space for rebellion to take root.

Observation:

Unhealed wounds in families often become open doors for spiritual rebellion.

Interpretation:

David's passivity as a father became the soil where Absalom's pride could grow.

The man who once conquered giants now had to confront his own household.

Theological Principle:

What you fail to confront in peace will rise to confront you in power.

The Conspiracy in the Kingdom

Absalom was handsome, charismatic, and cunning.

He began winning the hearts of the people by standing near the city gate, greeting citizens, and saying,

"See, thy matters are good and right; but there is no man deputed of the king to hear thee."

(2 Samuel 15:3)

Through subtle flattery and emotional manipulation, he stole the loyalty of Israel.

When his following grew strong enough, he declared himself king in Hebron—the very place where David had first been crowned.

Spiritual Insight:

Rebellion often begins at the gate of familiarity.

Absalom rose in the same city where David's humility was once rewarded—proof that every unguarded blessing can become an opportunity for betrayal.

The Flight of the King

When David heard of the conspiracy, he made no attempt to resist violently.

He told his servants,

"Arise, and let us flee; for we shall not else escape from Absalom." **(2 Samuel 15:14)**

Barefoot and weeping, he crossed the Brook Kidron and ascended the Mount of Olives—the same path Jesus would later take in His own sorrow.

The mighty king once celebrated by thousands now fled with a few loyal followers and the Ark trailing behind him.

But even in humiliation, David's heart returned to surrender.

He told the priests to take the Ark back to Jerusalem, saying,

"If I shall find favour in the eyes of the Lord, He will bring me again." **(2 Samuel 15:25)**

Observation:

David didn't cling to the symbol of God's presence—he trusted the God of the symbol.

Theological Principle:

When you've truly been formed by God, you can surrender what once defined you.

Spiritual Insight:

The wilderness that once broke him was now sanctifying him again.

David was learning that restoration sometimes requires returning to where you were first refined.

Ahithophel's Betrayal and Hushai's Loyalty

Among those who turned against David was **Ahithophel,** one of his most trusted counselors. Scripture says,

"The counsel of Ahithophel, which he counselled in those days, was as if a man had enquired at the oracle of God." **(2 Samuel 16:23)**

His advice once carried the weight of divine wisdom. But when Absalom rebelled, Ahithophel joined him—using his insight and strategy to plot against the king he had once served.

When David heard the news, his heart broke again. He cried out,

"O Lord, I pray thee, turn the counsel of Ahithophel into foolishness." **(2 Samuel 15:31)**

God immediately answered that prayer. David sent back his loyal friend **Hushai** into Absalom's camp, pretending to serve the new rebel king.

Hushai's mission was clear: to frustrate **Ahithophel's** counsel and protect David from within enemy lines.

When Absalom sought advice, Ahithophel urged immediate attack—swift and surgical, before David could regroup.

But Hushai suggested a delay, convincing
Absalom to gather all Israel for a larger battle.

Absalom followed Hushai's word instead—and
that hesitation gave David time to prepare,
fulfilling the very prayer he had prayed in
anguish.

Observation:

Even betrayal cannot outsmart divine providence.

Interpretation:

Ahithophel's wisdom failed not because he lost
his intelligence, but because God withdrew His
anointing from his words.

Theological Principle:

When the enemy's counsel sounds wise, prayer still has the final word.

Spiritual Insight:

Every servant of God will face betrayal by someone they once trusted. But for every Ahithophel who plots your fall, God has prepared a Hushai to protect your destiny.

Psychological Insight:

Ahithophel represents the wound of betrayal—when someone close uses their closeness to harm you.

Hushai represents God's faithfulness—proof that divine loyalty always outweighs human deceit.

Spiritual Principle:

The counsel of man can only stand until the prayer of the righteous speaks.

Ahithophel's end came tragically. When he saw that his advice was not followed, pride consumed him. He went home, set his affairs in order, and hanged himself **(2 Samuel 17:23).**

Even in death, he became a warning: pride turns wise men into fools, and rebellion ends in ruin.

Shimei's Cursing and David's Restraint

As David fled, a man named **Shimei** from Saul's tribe hurled stones and curses at him, shouting,

"Come out, thou bloody man, and thou man of Belial." (2 Samuel 16:7)

Abishai, one of David's warriors, wanted to strike him down.

But David stopped him, saying,

"Let him alone, and let him curse; for the Lord hath bidden him." **(2 Samuel 16:11)**

Observation:

Humiliation tests humility.

Interpretation:

David recognized that even insults can be instruments of God when you're in a season of refining.

Theological Principle:

When you stop defending yourself, God becomes your defender.

Spiritual Insight:

Maturity is not proven by how you fight your enemies, but by how you handle your critics.

Psalmic Reflection — Psalm 3: A Song in Exile

"Lord, how are they increased that trouble me! many are they that rise up against me...

But Thou, O Lord, art a shield for me; my glory, and the lifter up of mine head." **(Psalm 3:1, 3)**

Psalm 3 was written as David fled from Absalom.

It is one of the most personal cries in all Scripture—a king without a throne finding peace without a palace.

Interpretation:

Even when betrayed by his own blood, David remembered that God alone was his glory.

Theological Principle:

When man casts you down, only worship can lift you up.

Spiritual Insight:

The wilderness is where faith stops being positional and becomes personal again.

The Death of Absalom — The Pain of Victory

Eventually, Absalom's rebellion was crushed.

While fleeing the battle, his long hair caught in the branches of an oak tree, and he was left hanging—*symbolic of pride entangled in its own vanity.*

Joab, David's general, ignored the king's command to deal gently with the young man and killed him.

When the news reached David, he was undone.

"O my son Absalom, my son, my son Absalom! would God I had died for thee."

(2 Samuel 18:33)

Psychological and Spiritual Insight:

The deepest pain is not from your enemies—it's from those you raised.

But even this grief became part of David's refining. He learned that restoration does not erase consequences, yet mercy must remain the heartbeat of leadership.

Theological Principle:

Even in judgment, the love of a father reveals the heart of the Father.

Stage Insight

The Refinement Stage teaches that every level of blessing carries a corresponding test of brokenness.

God brings us back to familiar places of pain— not to shame us, but to remind us where our strength truly comes from.

David's first wilderness made him a warrior.

This wilderness made him a worshipper again.

He discovered that failure wasn't final, and that even when surrounded by rebellion, God still calls His servants by name.

Spiritual Insight:

God sometimes repeats your wilderness so He can deepen your worship.

Wisdom Keys

- The higher the call, the deeper the refinement.

- Unhealed pain in a family can become the breeding ground of rebellion.

- Humiliation handled well becomes holiness.

- You cannot defend your destiny and surrender to God at the same time.

- Betrayal reveals what loyalty conceals.

- God's grace can find you even when your crown cannot.

Reflective Questions:

1. What lessons from my first wilderness might God be reminding me of today?

2. Have I allowed comfort to weaken my discipline or devotion?

3. How do I respond when betrayal comes from those close to me?

4. Can I trust God to defend me when I'm falsely accused?

5. What does true repentance and surrender look like in this season of my life?

Reflection Summary:

David's story came full circle.

The same king who once fled from Saul now fled from his son.

But in this second wilderness, his posture changed—no longer angry, just surrendered.

He rediscovered that God's faithfulness is not proven by the absence of trouble, but by His presence in the midst of it.

Even the betrayal of Ahithophel and the rebellion of Absalom became tools in God's refining fire.

The king's heart was purified again, not on a throne, but on a dusty road of tears.

Prayer:

Lord,

When You bring me back to old wildernesses, remind me they are places of mercy, not punishment.

Teach me to bow instead of break, to worship instead of worry.

Let my heart remain teachable, even after triumph.

If my crown must fall for my character to rise, let it be so—

for You alone are my King.

In Jesus' name, Amen.

Chapter 11 – The Restoration of the King: Mercy, Maturity, and the Message of Grace

"And the king returned, and came to Jordan. And Judah came to Gilgal, to go to meet the king, to conduct the king over Jordan."

— 2 Samuel 19:15

The Maturity Stage — When Grace Finishes What Discipline Began

This marked **the eleventh stage** of David's development—**the Maturity Stage.**

By now, David had walked through triumph and tragedy, betrayal and restoration, sin and forgiveness.

He was no longer the shepherd boy chasing lions or the fugitive hiding in caves. He was a man remade by mercy—broken, wiser, and slower to speak.

God had used every victory, every wound, and every tear to form in him the one thing He values most: a heart that mirrors His own.

Spiritual Insight:

The man after God's own heart is not the one who never falls—it's the one who keeps returning.

Theological Principle:

The process of grace doesn't end at the throne; it continues in the heart.

Crossing Back Over Jordan

After Absalom's death, David remained in mourning until Joab confronted him:

"Thou hast shamed this day the faces of all thy servants, which this day have saved thy life."

(2 Samuel 19:5)

Joab's words stirred David to rise from grief and return to leadership.

The nation was divided—some loyal to Absalom's memory, others waiting for reconciliation. But slowly, the tribes of Israel came together again, saying,

"The king saved us out of the hand of our enemies... now therefore why speak ye not a word of bringing the king back?"

(2 Samuel 19:9–10)

So, David crossed the Jordan once more—not as a conquering warrior, but as a chastened king.

Every step toward Jerusalem was a reminder that restoration is not just God's mercy—it is God's mission.

Observation:

Grace doesn't erase scars; it redeems them.

Interpretation:

God didn't restore David because he was perfect. He restored him because he was purified.

Theological Principle:

The same God who humbles the proud lifts the broken.

Spiritual Insight:

Crossing Jordan symbolized a spiritual return— the crossing back from shame to purpose, from discipline to destiny.

Mercy to Shimei — The Fruit of Refinement

Among those who came to meet David was **Shimei,** the man who had cursed him on his way out of Jerusalem.

Now trembling and remorseful, Shimei bowed before the king and begged for forgiveness.

Abishai, ever zealous, said, *"Shall not Shimei be put to death for this?"*

But David, now a changed man, answered:

"What have I to do with you, ye sons of Zeruiah, that ye should this day be adversaries unto me? Shall there any man be put to death this day in Israel? for do not I know that I am this day king over Israel?" **(2 Samuel 19:22)**

David forgave him.

Observation:

Restoration gives you the strength to show mercy to those who once mocked you.

Interpretation:

David was no longer fighting to prove he was king. He was at peace with who God made him.

Spiritual Insight:

When you know you've been forgiven, you no longer crave revenge.

Mercy becomes the proof of maturity.

Theological Principle:

Authority without humility becomes tyranny; but authority shaped by grace becomes peace.

Mephibosheth's Loyalty and Ziba's Deception

As David returned, Mephibosheth also came to meet him. His feet were unwashed, his clothes unchanged—a sign of mourning.

When David asked why he had not fled with him, Mephibosheth explained that Ziba, his servant, had deceived him and slandered his loyalty.

David listened, then divided the land between them.

It was a moment of divine irony: the man who once received unearned favor now suffered undeserved suspicion.

Observation:

Even after restoration, not every misunderstanding is resolved.

Interpretation:

God sometimes allows tension to remain so humility can stay rooted.

Spiritual Insight:

Grace doesn't always vindicate you immediately—it keeps you quiet until time does.

Barzillai the Gileadite — The Blessing of the Faithful

Among the crowd was **Barzillai,** the elderly man who had supported David during his exile.

When David invited him to live in the palace, **Barzillai** declined, saying,

"I am this day fourscore years old… let thy servant, I pray thee, turn back again, that I may die in mine own city." **(2 Samuel 19:35–37)**

Barzillai's faithfulness reminded David that true friends are not made in comfort, but in crisis.

He blessed him and ensured his household would be honored for generations.

Theological Principle:

God always rewards those who refresh His servants in their season of weakness.

Spiritual Insight:

Restoration is not complete until gratitude is expressed to those who stood by you in exile.

Psalmic Reflection — Psalm 30: A Song of Restoration

"O Lord my God, I cried unto thee, and thou hast healed me. Thou hast turned for me my mourning into dancing: thou hast put off my sackcloth, and girded me with gladness."

(Psalm 30:2, 11)

Psalm 30 is David's heart song of renewal—a declaration that discipline does not destroy the righteous, but refines them.

This psalm embodies the journey from sorrow to song, from weeping to worship.

Interpretation:

David's mourning had purpose; his restoration
had praise.

Theological Principle:

The same God who disciplines in darkness
delights in bringing joy at dawn.

Spiritual Insight:

Every tear becomes oil for worship when
surrendered to the grace of God.

Stage Insight

The Maturity Stage teaches that grace is not a shortcut around pain—it's the strength to walk through it without losing heart.

David's return to the throne wasn't about power; it was about perspective.

He no longer ruled to prove himself, but to point others to the mercy of God.

The fire that once purified him now burned in his compassion.

He learned to forgive more easily, to listen more deeply, and to judge more righteously.

Spiritual Principle:

The sign of true maturity is not that you've stopped struggling, but that you've learned to worship while you wait.

Wisdom Keys

- Grace restores what pride destroys.

- True leadership forgives without forgetting the lesson.

- Restoration begins when repentance is complete.

- Those who show mercy reveal that they've met Mercy Himself.

- God finishes His work in you through the people you once overlooked.

Reflective Questions:

1. What has God taught me through my seasons of loss and restoration?

2. How can I show mercy to those who wronged me during my exile?

3. What "Barzillais" has God sent to bless me—and have I thanked them?

4. In what ways has discipline produced maturity in me?

5. Am I ruling my life from pride—or from the place of grace?

Reflection Summary:

David's restoration was not a return to the old, but the unveiling of the new.

The man who once fell to temptation now stood as a teacher of mercy.

His scars became his sermons; his pain became his praise.

In forgiving Shimei, honoring Barzillai, and trusting God's timing, David proved that grace had finished its work.

He had been anointed, broken, chased, betrayed, humbled—and now restored.

The wilderness was behind him, but worship remained before him.

And through his story, we see that the making of a man of God is never finished until mercy becomes his message.

Prayer:

Lord,

Thank You for restoring me when I deserved rejection.

Teach me to forgive as freely as You forgave me.

Help me see discipline not as punishment, but as preparation.

Make me a vessel of grace—steady, merciful, and wise.

When others see my scars, let them see Your mercy.

In Jesus' name, Amen.

Chapter 12 – Preparing the Next Generation: Passing the Mantle to Solomon

"And he charged Solomon his son, saying, I go the way of all the earth: be thou strong therefore, and shew thyself a man; and keep the charge of the Lord thy God."

— 1 Kings 2:1–3

The Legacy Stage — When the Work Becomes Worship

This final stage of David's development—**the Legacy Stage**—was not about battle or survival. It was about impartation.

The man who once led armies was now leading hearts.

David had discovered that his greatest victory was not the defeat of Goliath, nor the unification of Israel, but the transfer of wisdom to the next generation.

He was now an old man—his hair silvered, his body weakened, but his spirit alive with vision.

He had been a warrior, a worshipper, a king, and a father.

Now, he became a mentor and prophet, preparing Solomon to rule in righteousness and wisdom.

Spiritual Insight:

The proof that God has truly formed you is not in what you build, but in who you prepare.

Theological Principle:

Every man of God must eventually become a father in God.

Establishing Order Before Departure

Before David died, he set his house and kingdom in order.

He organized the Levites, assigned the priests, gathered materials for the temple, and appointed singers for worship **(1 Chronicles 23–25).**

He didn't wait for Solomon to start what he could still prepare.

He taught his son that **worship** is the foundation of leadership and that **obedience** is the measure of success.

"Now set your heart and your soul to seek the Lord your God; arise therefore, and build ye the sanctuary of the Lord God."

(1 Chronicles 22:19)

Observation:

A wise man doesn't just leave wealth—he leaves order.

Interpretation:

David's greatest building project was not the temple—it was the next generation of worshippers.

Theological Principle:

Legacy is not what you leave to people, but what you leave in them.

Spiritual Insight:

God will finish through your successors what He began in your surrender.

The Charge to Solomon

As the day of his departure drew near, David called Solomon close and gave him the charge that still echoes across the centuries:

"Be thou strong therefore, and shew thyself a man; and keep the charge of the Lord thy God, to walk in His ways, to keep His statutes… that thou mayest prosper in all that thou doest."

(1 Kings 2:2–3)

David knew that kingship without character would collapse.

He warned Solomon to walk in obedience, to remember mercy, and to fear the Lord.

He spoke as a father who had tasted failure and grace in equal measure.

Observation:

Only a man who has fallen can teach the next generation how to stand.

Interpretation:

David's scars were now his sermons. His mistakes became lessons Solomon would not have to repeat.

Theological Principle:

God redeems your past so you can protect someone else's future.

Spiritual Insight:

Mature faith doesn't hide its wounds—it uses them to heal others.

The Offering for the House of God

Though David was forbidden to build the temple, he spent his final years gathering resources for it—*gold, silver, iron, cedar,* and *stone* in abundance.

"Now I have prepared with all my might for the house of my God." **(1 Chronicles 29:2)**

Then he made a public offering and led Israel in giving. His joy was no longer in conquest but in contribution.

He rejoiced that his son would complete what he could only begin.

Spiritual Insight:

A man of God dies content when he sees others stepping into what he once dreamed.

Theological Principle:

Your ceiling should become their floor.

Psalmic Reflection — Psalm 72: A Prayer for Solomon

"Give the king thy judgments, O God, and thy righteousness unto the king's son... He shall judge thy people with righteousness, and thy poor with judgment." **(Psalm 72:1–2)**

Psalm 72, attributed to David, is both prayer and prophecy. It expresses his desire that Solomon's reign would reflect *the justice, mercy,* and *peace* of God Himself.

It reveals a father's final intercession—a man who had learned that the kingdom is safest when ruled by divine wisdom.

Interpretation:

Even in death, David's greatest act of leadership was prayer.

Theological Principle:

True kings don't just raise successors—they intercede for them.

David's Final Words

David's final recorded words summarize the heart of his journey:

"He that ruleth over men must be just, ruling in the fear of God... although my house be not so with God; yet He hath made with me an everlasting covenant." **(2 Samuel 23:3, 5)**

He died knowing that God's covenant would outlive his failures.

The boy who once sang to sheep had become a man who sang to nations—and now left behind a *son, a kingdom,* and *a song* that would never die.

Spiritual Insight:

When you've been through the making, you no longer fear the leaving.

Stage Insight

The Legacy Stage teaches that every calling must become a commission.

David's story closes not with a crown on his head but with a prayer on his lips.

He leaves behind *worship, wisdom,* and *the witness* that God keeps covenant to a thousand generations.

The fire that once tested him now burns in Solomon's temple.

The tears that once stained his wilderness now water the next generation's faith.

He learned that the making of a man of God does not end with personal victory—it ends with generational vision.

Spiritual Principle:

God's greatest work through you begins when you start preparing others to take your place.

Wisdom Keys

- A true leader prepares before he departs.

- Legacy is built in the small acts of obedience that outlive us.

- God finishes through your sons what He began through your surrender.

- Your greatest investment is not gold—it's godliness.

- A man of God measures success by faithfulness, not fame.

Reflective Questions:

1. Who am I intentionally preparing to carry God's work forward?

2. What wisdom has my pain taught me that I can pass on to others?

3. Have I made peace with the limits of my own calling?

4. What resources—spiritual or practical— am I storing for those who will follow me?

5. When I leave this world, what will remain that points others to God's faithfulness?

Reflection Summary:

David's journey began with a sling and ended with a song.

He walked through rejection, warfare, sin, repentance, and restoration—only to discover that God's mercy outlasts every mistake.

He died not in shame, but in peace—knowing that his life had become the melody of grace.

From the pasture to the palace, from caves to covenant, David's story proves one eternal truth:

The making of a man of God is the making of a worshipper.

Everything else—thrones, crowns, and kingdoms—will fade, but the heart that bows in surrender will echo through eternity.

Prayer:

Lord,

Thank You for every lesson that shaped me, every trial that refined me, and every mercy that restored me.

Help me to finish well—not in pride, but in purpose.

Show me how to prepare others to serve You with greater strength and purity.

May my words, my works, and my worship point future generations back to You.

In Jesus' name, Amen.

Epilogue – Still Being Made

David's story reminds us that God's greatest work is not done through us, but in us.

The shepherd who became a king was never a finished product—he was a continual work of grace.

He failed, but he never quit seeking.

He fell, but he always rose to worship.

And through every season—*caves, crowns,* and *tears*—God kept shaping his heart.

The same God who made David a man after His own heart is still at work today, forming His sons and daughters in hidden places.

He uses *rejection* to teach trust, *pain* to purify motives, and *success* to test surrender.

The process never stops; it only deepens.

"Being confident of this very thing, that He which hath begun a good work in you will perform it until the day of Jesus Christ."

(Philippians 1:6)

So, if you find yourself in the wilderness again, take courage.

You are not being punished—you are being perfected.

The making of a man of God never ends until His image is fully seen in you.

Final Benediction

May the God who anointed David anoint you also— to stand in your calling, to endure your wilderness, and to finish your race in faith.

May every trial refine you; every setback strengthen you, and every victory remind you of His grace.

May your worship never fade, your heart never harden, and your faith never fail.

And when your life's song is complete, may it be said that you were a man or woman after God's own heart.

In the name of the Father, the Son, and the Holy Ghost—Amen.

Your Turn in the Making

Every believer will walk through the same seasons that shaped David— not to become famous, but to become faithful.

You may be in your **Anointing Stage**, where God has called you but the world hasn't noticed.

Or perhaps you're in the **Wilderness Stage,** where you're being tested and refined in secret.

Maybe you're in the **Refinement Stage,** learning to trust again after failure or loss.

Or you may stand in your **Restoration Stage,** where grace has lifted you back to purpose.

Wherever you are, take heart— the same God who began the work is still completing it in you.

- He anoints the overlooked.

- He strengthens the weary.

- He restores the broken.

- And He finishes what He starts.

Your story is still being written.

Let every trial teach you.

Let every blessing humble you.

And let every breath be praise to the God who makes men and women after His own heart.

"For the Lord seeth not as man seeth; for man looketh on the outward appearance, but the Lord looketh on the heart."

— 1 Samuel 16:7

Heavy Is the Head That Wears the Crown

A Call to Responsibility

Every crown carries a cost. Before God places a crown upon a man's head, He first places a cross upon his back. The path to leadership is paved with lessons in humility, obedience, and endurance. The anointing may come in a moment, but the preparation takes a lifetime.

The crown is not a symbol of honor alone—it is a weight of accountability. To be chosen by God is to be set apart, refined through pressure, and proven in private before being revealed in public. David's story reminds us that true kingship begins in obscurity, not in the palace.

He learned responsibility in the pasture, courage in the valley, and restraint in the cave. God shaped him through service, solitude, and surrender. Every battle, betrayal, and breakthrough prepared him for the throne—not to glorify himself, but to glorify God.

Heavy indeed is the head that wears the crown. For to lead is not to rule, but to serve. The one who bows before God in secret is the only one fit to stand before men in power.

So, when God elevates you, remember this truth:

The weight of the crown is not found in gold—it rests in the call to carry God's heart with integrity.

About the Author

Eld Joel Latimore Jr. is a Spirit-filled author, teacher, and U.S. Army veteran whose writings inspire believers to embrace the refining process of God with faith, humility, and perseverance.

Through years of ministry, mentorship, and personal transformation, he has learned that true strength is not found in titles or triumphs but in total surrender to the will of God.

Known for his prophetic insight and devotion to holiness, Elder Latimore writes with passion and precision—helping readers recognize that the trials which break us are often the very tools God uses to build us.

His books, including Faith and Fire: Walking with the Holy Ghost and You Were Born for More, challenge the body of Christ to move beyond comfort into spiritual maturity, obedience, and power.

Elder Latimore is the founder of Latimore Publishing, a ministry dedicated to producing faith-based literature that restores integrity, inspires purpose, and rekindles devotion to the Word of God.

His life and work continue to remind believers everywhere that before God crowns a man, He must first crush him into His image.

He resides in Cleveland, Ohio, where he continues to write, teach, and mentor others in their walk with Christ.

www.ingramcontent.com/pod-product-compliance
Lightning Source LLC
Chambersburg PA
CBHW071138130626
46553CB00004B/1424